# SOWN IN THE STARS

Sarah L. Hall

# SOWN IN THE STARS

## Planting by the Signs

PHOTOGRAPHS BY
Meg Wilson

UNIVERSITY PRESS OF KENTUCKY

FOREWORD BY
Ronni Lundy

Copyright © 2023 by The University Press of Kentucky

Scholarly publisher for the Commonwealth, serving Bellarmine University, Berea College, Centre College of Kentucky, Eastern Kentucky University, The Filson Historical Society, Georgetown College, Kentucky Historical Society, Kentucky State University, Morehead State University, Murray State University, Northern Kentucky University, Spalding University, Transylvania University, University of Kentucky, University of Louisville, University of Pikeville, and Western Kentucky University.

***Editorial and Sales Offices:*** The University Press of Kentucky
663 South Limestone Street, Lexington, Kentucky 40508-4008
**www.kentuckypress.com**

This volume offers an overview of beliefs and practices associated with planting by the signs and is not intended as a guide to food preparation, agriculture, or health care. Information drawn from interviews should be understood as opinion. Readers attempting to use this information for their own purposes are advised that the author and publisher do not accept responsibility for the outcome.

Cataloging-in-Publication data is available from the Library of Congress.

ISBN 978-0-8131-9704-3 (hardcover : alk. paper)
ISBN 978-0-8131-9706-7 (epub)
ISBN 978-0-8131-9705-0 (pdf)

This book is printed on acid-free paper meeting
the requirements of the American National Standard
for Permanence in Paper for Printed Library Materials. ♾

*Manufactured in the United States of America.*

Member of the Association of University Presses.

For my granny, Zelma Lee Hall,
and for John Clay;
without either of them,
this project would not have grown.

And for the countless folks in Kentucky and beyond
who are keeping this rich tradition alive and well.

# CONTENTS

# Author's Note

Interviews for this project took place during 2018–2019. Between then and now, some of the people I interviewed have passed. I am especially grateful I got to spend a brief time with each of them: Jess Clarkson Jr. (1924–2021), Abby Turner Walker (1965–2021), Anita Baker Tolliver (1958–2022), and Clyde Charles (1934–2021). I hope their loved ones find some solace in their words and lessons documented here and in their recorded interviews.

# Foreword

THE SUMMER I TURNED EIGHT, A LARGE AND ugly wart appeared on my right knee. My mother warned me not to touch it and to be careful not to scrape it or make it bleed, for fear that it could spread. She dosed it with some drops from the drugstore and later with a paste of wet baking soda; she even tried a dab of the prescription fungal cream my father used to treat his athlete's foot. Nothing worked to rid me of the blemish, and by the time August rolled up, the wart had started to have babies—tiny warts in a disagreeable constellation around it.

But August also brought my father's vacation and our summer trip up home to Corbin, Kentucky, and the Lundy reunion. It was there that my mother led me to a chair under one of the big trees at Levi Jackson Park where my father's oldest brother, Brownell, sat. In the absence of my grandparents, who had both died when my father was but a child, Brownell was head of the family and, despite his kindly smile, someone who awed both myself and my mother. I suppose that's why, when he told her to wait for the full moon, cut a potato in half, rub it on my warts, and then bury it somewhere no one could find it, that is exactly what she did a week later. And lo, within days that wart and all its wicked little satellites were completely gone.

It's decades now since Brownell passed on and nearly that long that I have regretted not sitting down with him when I was a bit older and asking what else he knew about the power of the moon and the nature of the signs. I expect my great-aunts Johnnie and Ray, who planted a huge garden that burst with tomatoes, cucumbers, and enough green beans to eat all summer and dry for the winter, might have had some things to tell me as well. And that is one reason I am so grateful that Sarah Hall has done the work to cover my loss—and then some!

At the heart of *Sown in the Stars: Planting by the Signs* you will find interviews (and delightful photographs by Meg Wilson) with nearly two dozen contemporary Kentuckians who still follow the signs of the moon and the stars to plant, preserve, cure, and perform other works of living. If their stories remind you of similar ones from the elders interviewed in the Foxfire books, it's worth noting that the first volume of that series, which also included "planting by the signs" as part of the title, was published in 1972. Nothing in the half century of agricultural and technological progress since then has dissuaded anyone here in their beliefs.

But *Sown in the Stars* is much more than a collection of oral histories. At the outset, Sarah explores the roots of this belief system in both astrology and astronomy. Neither a science nor a method of magic, sign systems might best be interpreted as a language indicative of the profound connections our ancestors felt to the stars, moon, and planets above them and the earth they lived on below. It's a language we stand to lose as we increasingly encase our lives in metal and concrete, our eyes and attention focused on machines. The history and mystery of the signs ask us to consider whether planting—indeed, living— in conversation and harmony with the vast natural world around us might provide much more than bumper crops and perfectly fermented sour corn.

Should you decide that you want to try it and see, this wonderful book provides a guide to the sometimes bewildering possibilities in the Almanacs and Calendars chapter. As Sarah notes, "Comparing various calendars, each of which claims to be the most accurate, reveals enough similarities to make a person believe, but enough differences to let a bit of doubt peek through the cracks." Even among the interviewees quoted here, and even among families, interpreting the benefits and drawbacks of specific signs may yield contradictory results.

To help us sort through the possibilities, Sarah gives us an in-depth guide to the many almanacs and calendars that are still published and still popular among adherents. And then she collates and considers all the information she has gleaned—from interviews as well as written sources—and compiles it into a comprehensive, comprehendible, and delightfully useful guide to the signs for everything from planting cucumbers to harvesting hay to castrating cattle to getting dental work done. Then, like a good friend, she thoughtfully brings this remarkable book to a close with an honest appraisal of her own work with the signs—most of it successful, some of it not quite, but all of it rich in the awareness of the world around and within.

So, did Uncle Brownell perform magic that summer long ago? I can only answer maybe. But I can tell you with certainty that this book you hold in your hand is pure magic indeed.

**Ronni Lundy**
OCTOBER 2021

# Introduction

*Everything on Earth is actually only a reflection of what is taking place in the cosmos. This fact is hidden with human beings, because we have emancipated ourselves; we carry only the inner rhythms within us. The plants, however, are still very much a reflection of the cosmos.*

RUDOLF STEINER, *Agriculture*

EVERY SUNDAY OF MY CHILDHOOD, WE WOULD GO to church in the morning, then head to my granny's place for the rest of the day. That drive took me from relatively flat central Kentucky into the rolling hills of the Knobs—the transition into the Appalachian Mountains. My granny lived in Estill County, along a ridge-top known as Sand Hill, a stone's throw from a big curve in the Kentucky River. My memories of those days are incredibly rich. They were filled with explorations in the woods that fostered in me a desire to learn and understand more about the complexities of the natural world. The smells coming from the stove and the oven were always plentiful and foreshadowed tastes that testified to my granny's skill as a cook. Her ability to cover the stovetop and fill the oven without a single missed step continues to leave me in awe, as I sometimes struggle to make half the number of dishes she did. My cousins became my friends as we explored the pastures, forests, and creek surrounding us. I heard stories while breaking beans or peeling apples that implanted family roots from a very different time. One that still sticks out in my mind is my granny's argument with the electric company about cutting down some sugar maple trees my grandfather, who had died well before then, had so caringly planted.

Another thing I remember is the gardens I saw on our drive to my granny's. Freshly plowed soil marked the coming spring more consistently than any date on the calendar, school vacation, or even Easter. The newly exposed soil declared to everyone that there would be sweat and toil to come, but most of all, there would be food. The further we got from the highway, the denser those blank garden canvases became. As the spring wore on, the "paint" appeared, and occasionally a gardening artist could be spotted at work. I took note of the different styles of gardening and wondered about some of the plants I didn't recognize. I noticed how each garden had its own character or personality, a reflection of the artists themselves; some plots were meticulously groomed and orderly (with staked strings to ensure straight rows during planting), while others were a bit more free-form and whimsical. The structures for supporting beans varied greatly; many featured tobacco sticks as the primary structure (sometimes with strings attached), while others used long bamboo poles or branches recovered from the forest floor. Each garden had a unique arrangement that was perfect in its own way. One thing I knew for sure was that just like the garden at my granny's, those rows of vegetables would become staples for winter meals, stored wherever there was space, whether on a shelf or under a bed, to provide nourishment while the garden slept. And as the winter progressed, the once-filled jars would be replaced with empties, ready for next year's harvest.

☆ ☆ ☆

Twelve years ago, while I was working at the Kentucky State University research farm, a man stopped by and gave me a bag of seeds. He told me they were from a "mushmelon" his family had brought from Arkansas and said if I planted them under a certain sign, they would go an inch deeper in the soil than at any other time. I tucked that advice away in the back of my mind, like the little bag of seeds he gave me, which was buried in my seed box and forgotten. During the fall semesters of 2013 and 2015 I developed and taught a new course at Berea College entitled Appalachian Plants and People, which allowed me to combine my interests in native plants and Appalachian traditions and customs.[1] I originally intended to focus only on native plants used for medicine, food, or craft, but it became apparent from a number of student projects that agricultural crops and practices, especially those traditions being lost over time, should also be included.

As I explored resources on agricultural traditions, I became fascinated with the practice of planting by the moon or the zodiac signs. This topic was discussed in some of my course materials, but I was surprised not to see it referenced in more places. For instance, some films produced by Appalshop focused on medicinals and wildcrafting, but they largely told the stories of the people they highlighted and, to a lesser extent, the materials they used.[2] The Appalshop films on agriculture tended to focus on the mechanics of farming, changes in the economy, and how those changes have impacted farmers.[3] None highlighted the traditional practice of planting by the signs, despite the fact that it is a fairly well-known custom (at least by name). The practice is covered in a chapter of *The Foxfire Book* and a few pages of *Foxfire 11*.[4] I was surprised at the lack of materials I found in the cultural record, given the importance of this tradition.

Some context is provided by Gerald Milnes, who writes of the rich religious history of Appalachia and the connection to astronomy and astrology: "Ancient Germanic cosmology tied to theology is inherent in Appalachian folklore. The relationship of man to the natural world . . . flourished as the strongest expression of folk art in the New World." In his chapter "Witchery on the Farm," Milnes writes, "Traditional rural life touches on many misunderstood natural and biological laws and forces. . . . Luck is not an arbitrary entity; good fortune is assisted through adherence to a cosmology and magical thought process that has stood the test of time."[5]

It does seem (even to a scientist like me) that when a practice continues over a long period of time, there might just be something to it. When I asked David Cooke, former director of Grow Appalachia, whether he hears farmers or gardeners talk about planting by the signs, he responded, "I believe many people still plant by the signs and it is a lively source of discussion every year within Grow Appalachia."[6] The time I spent initially researching the subject only piqued my interest and led me to the conclusion that a significant number of people are still following the tradition and could enrich the historical record even more.

In contrast to the apparent paucity of information on individual stories and culture, there are numerous how-to guides on planting by the signs.[7] The use of various farmers' almanacs and related calendars is rooted in the practice. Milnes provides a good overview of astrology and the "almanac man," whose image still appears in many of these publications.[8] A Tennessee company prints calendars depicting the astrological signs and customizes them with advertisements for different businesses, which distribute the calendars to their customers throughout Appalachia. I remember seeing these calendars at my granny's house in Estill County when I was growing up. Even closer to home in central Kentucky, a widely distributed calendar (available at Good Foods Co-op in Lexington and at Happy Meadow in Berea) shows when the signs occur and provides clear information about what should be done and avoided during those times.[9] That these guides and calendars are still in use today is evidence of contemporary interest in the subject.

Finally, I turned my attention to the scientific literature, assuming some studies must have been done on the practice. But after a few hours of looking, I had discovered only two articles and one book chapter.[10] It wasn't much, but all three sources provided some evidence that plant growth can be affected by the moon, and my interest in the subject was strengthened. (I have since learned from Susana Lein, one of the farmers I interviewed, of Maria Thun's work, which provides a very strong case for following this practice.[11] Thun conducted controlled growth trials at her home in Germany. This resulted in the development of the biodynamic calendar, which relies on the zodiac signs and is followed today by many biodynamic gardeners and farmers.) As I began to think about the possibilities for my sabbatical during

the 2018–2019 academic year, the idea of interviewing people who plant by the signs and collecting their stories was clearly high on my list. When I pulled out my seed box in 2017 to see what I might like to plant, I ran across the bag of melon seeds marked "Mr. Clay, KSU Farm, 2010." That was the last sign I needed.

Planting by the signs is an important practice in Appalachia. While it may be less common today than it was in the past, it could help our current agricultural and food systems become more resilient in the face of a changing climate. This is part of why I am interested in the subject. I am also interested because I love Appalachia. I

Mushmelon grown by the author from the seeds John Clay gave her in 2010.

wanted to collect the stories of people who still use or remember using this practice in my Kentucky home. This project marries my interest in Appalachian plants and people with a focus on this specific agricultural practice, which, in my opinion, has received inadequate attention and is in danger of being lost with the passing of older folks. This project also gave me an opportunity to sit down and learn from a handful of the numerous garden artists who fill the spring and summer palettes of the Kentucky landscape with their unique work.

The garden at my granny's was always a communal effort; there was never a singular artist. My uncle largely prepared and planted it, with help from my cousins and my father. When it was time for harvesting and processing, everyone pitched in—my cousins, sisters, aunts, and uncles. In the same way, this project was a communal effort. I found my way to the people featured herein largely via word of mouth through my Berea contacts and by fostering networks with Grow Appalachia and the Pine Mountain and Hindman Settlement Schools. These organizations and their programs were crucial in building bridges to several of the people interviewed.

It is no secret that Appalachia and its people have often been portrayed through a less than flattering lens. To those who deeply love their home and their way of life, allowing a stranger in (along with a voice recorder and a camera, no less!) is a large ask. Despite this, I was repeatedly met with warmth, pride, and an eagerness to share. With this book, it is my intention to present both the people who participated and this fascinating practice with deep respect. I couldn't possibly capture the complexity of the lived experiences of each individual within these pages, but I have done my best to provide a small glimpse and to pass on what they shared with me. I am greatly indebted to all those who allowed me into their homes or gardens and added their voices to this project.

I still go to my granny's place occasionally, although she is no longer with us. Some of those fully painted garden canvases I remember from my childhood are still evident on the drive, and some new ones have appeared. But many are no longer there. This project was my opportunity to get a behind-the-scenes look into the skills, knowledge, and stories of those who are growing food and keeping tradition alive in Appalachia. In some cases, the artists were no longer able to paint their own garden canvases, but their memories were still fresh enough to share the process with the rest of us. In other cases, I was able to witness the painting in progress during a snapshot in time. One thing I noted in all my interviews was that women were responsible for handing down the practice of planting by the signs. Most of the men I interviewed had been taught by their wives, mothers, or grandmothers. And for the women I interviewed, it was the same: they learned the practice from the women in their lives.

There are, of course, countless other garden artists not included in this book. If you know some of them, I hope you take the time to ask them questions, listen to their stories, and record them yourself. And I hope everyone reading this book will be inspired to get out and put some seeds in the ground or in a tub of potting soil on the porch. While written text and audio recordings are powerful tools in preserving this art, there is even more to be said for the act of getting out and becoming an artist yourself.

# The Basics

Spend some time around people who have been gardening or farming for a while, and you're likely to hear someone suggest that you wait to plant those seeds in your hand or ask what the "signs" were when you set those fence poles that are now leaning. You also might hear a bunch of other remarks you write off as superstition and nonsense. But then you hear the same comments from someone whose immaculate garden is teeming with tender, juicy vegetables that show no signs of damage from those pesky insects plaguing your garden. At another house you notice a red and black calendar with strange-looking symbols hanging on the wall, and when you ask your acquaintance to explain what it all means, she tells you the Head is a killing sign, the Breast is good for just about anything, but don't ever do your kraut or any kind of preserving when the signs are in the Bowels. And she says, "For your beans, now, you want to plant them in the Arms."

## ASTROLOGY VERSUS ASTRONOMY

A brief overview of astrology and astronomy is warranted to provide the basic contexts of planting by the signs. A little bit of knowledge about these topics can also help answer questions that might arise when comparing different calendars or almanacs (essential tools for the practice). More than one of the individuals interviewed made sure to distinguish their planting routines from the beliefs of those who follow astrology, but clearly there are common historical and philosophical roots.

Both astrology and astronomy seek to make sense of the stars, the planets, the sun, and the moon. And both use what is known about the present to predict the future. Astrology predates astronomy and has been around for essentially all of

human history for which there is a written record. The two fields share a history for much of that time, so it is not surprising that it can be difficult to separate them.

The Babylonians are credited with creating astrology in around the second millennium BCE.[1] They were limited by the tools and knowledge of their time, which meant their observations were based on what they could see with their eyes. Over a number of centuries, they made observations and measurements that contributed to the development of a calendar system as well as a set of beliefs or omens. These omens posited that certain stellar, planetary, lunar, or solar positions were correlated with events on earth, such as weather phenomena, crop failures, or the death of a king. Belief in these omens was based on the idea that divine beings communicated through the heavens—in other words, the gods used the heavenly bodies to communicate with those on earth.[2] Astrology was a religious belief system, and diviners were tasked with finding patterns and conveying them to the king. The Babylonian calendar used the lunar and solar cycles, with each month consisting of a thirty-day cycle and each year having twelve months.

Astronomy is the study of the celestial bodies or objects in the sky. The only predictions it makes are those based on the placement of certain entities and their interactions with one another, such as the occurrence of lunar and solar eclipses and high and low tides. Astronomy does not make predictions about human behavior or the outcomes of haircuts, surgical procedures, business dealings, and the like. Those are in the realm of astrology. Astronomy is built on the foundation of astrology, but it arose when people noticed differences between what astrology purported to be true and their own observations of celestial bodies. The earliest records related to astronomy are the names of stars recorded in Sumerian records from Mesopotamia around the first millennium BCE. Thus, astrology and astronomy have geographic and temporal roots that are fairly close. Astronomical knowledge and tools advanced in many different parts of the world over thousands of years.

Over that same long period, astrology continued as well, and its predictions became more specific, expanding into the realm of individual and collective behavior and even medical outcomes. Astrology was enhanced by the Greeks and then by the Romans, but with the rise of Christianity, astrology became more or less condemned in areas where Christianity reigned.[3] Many astrological beliefs (and the clay tablets of the *Enuma Anu Enlil* itself) made their way to the Arab world.[4] Even as various religious traditions were established (rendering the celestial gods irrelevant), none offered astrology's specific guidance about daily activities, such as when to plant or

**FACING**
Bill Best's Noble beans.

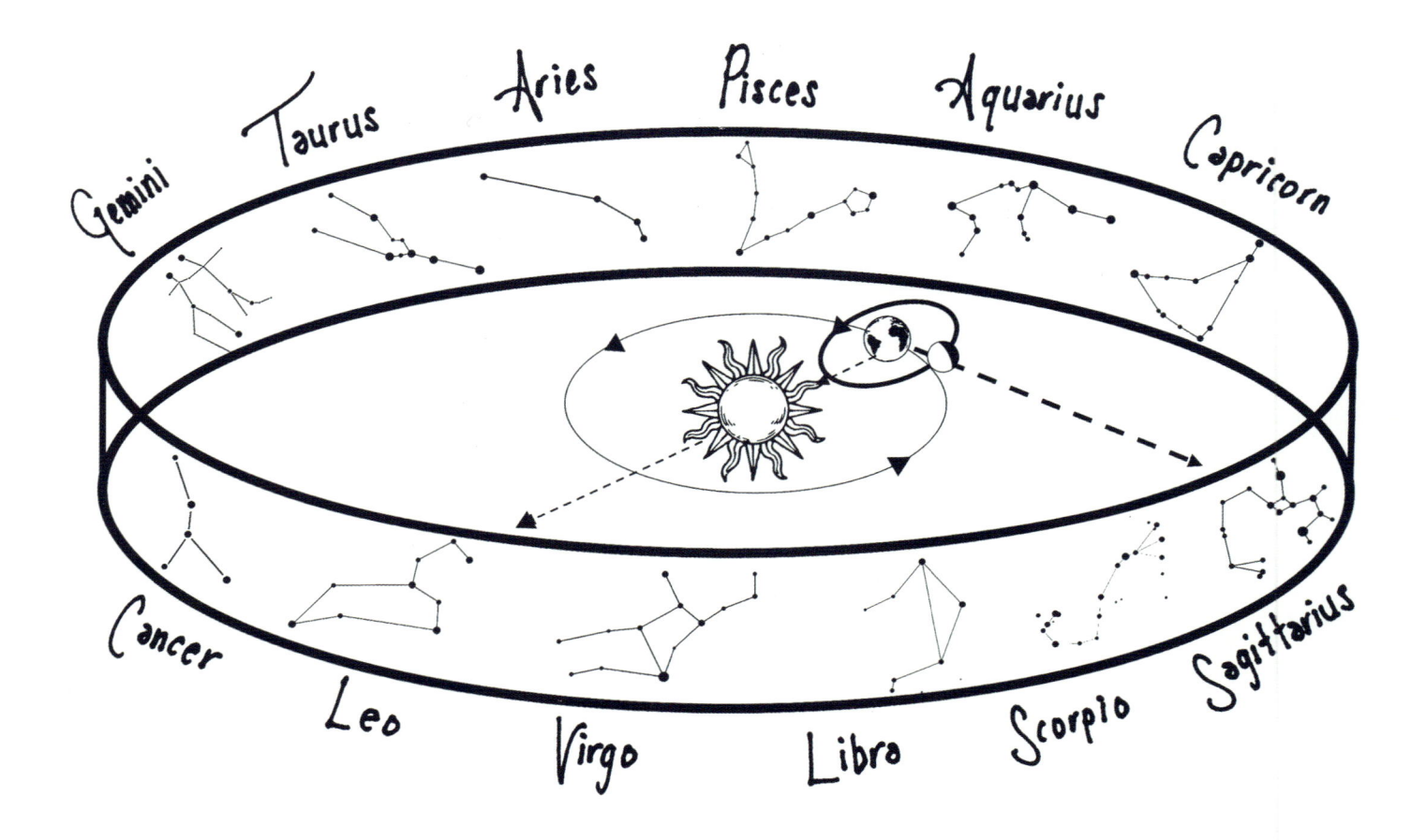

**FIGURE 1.1.** The ecliptic, or zodiacal belt, with the twelve constellations that make up the zodiac. The earth is shown on its annual orbit around the sun (inner thin solid line), when astronomers would say Leo is in superior conjunction to the sun and astrologers would say the sun sign is in Leo (from approximately July 23 through August 22). It also shows the moon's (approximately) monthly orbit around the earth (inner thick solid line), when the moon sign is in (or the moon is aspected to) Sagittarius. This means that, from the perspective of earth, the stars that form Leo are behind or obscured by the sun (thin dashed line), and the stars that form Sagittarius are behind the moon (thick dashed line). The moon is shown in the second quarter (waxing gibbous). *Illustration by Heather Dent.*

harvest crops. In addition, astrology had a long oral tradition, and countless generations had passed on their practices. During the seventeenth century, astronomy became a respected scholarly field, and astrology was relegated to pseudoscience status. But interest remained high, and astrology experienced a popular resurgence in the twentieth century, as evidenced by the inclusion of horoscopes in newspapers. With such a deep history and overlap with astronomy, it is not surprising that many people continued to believe in astrology (or some parts of it).

## THE ZODIAC

Early observations confirmed that the sun appeared to move along a certain path during the earth's 365-day year.[5] The moon's orbit around the earth, as well as the movement of other planets, appeared to follow the same path. This was evident by the sighting of different patterns of stars, or constellations, near the moon at different times during its (approximately) monthly revolution. Around the fifth century BCE, the Babylonians designated this path, which extended 8 degrees above and below the sun's path, and divided the entire belt into twelve 30-degree slices of the 365-degree pie. They named the stellar constellations within the belt based on the shapes they resembled (nearly all of which were animals), and they called the belt the zodiac.[6]

When considering the differences and similarities between astrology and astronomy, the zodiac is a great case study. Astronomers and astrologers agree that the earth orbits the sun in an ecliptic and that the moon orbits the earth in approximately the same plane. They also agree that within the zodiacal belt there are collections of stars that can be identified as the named constellations. However, the astronomer will point out that the "widths" of these constellations differ (thus, precise 30-degree increments are irrelevant) and that there are additional constellations within the zodiac besides the twelve used by astrologers. The astronomer will also point out that due to the precession of the equinoxes, the constellations are no longer oriented to the earth and the sun in the same way they were when the Babylonians envisioned the zodiac.

## PRECESSION OF THE EQUINOXES

The earth is not perfectly spherical; it is oblate or bulged in the middle (at the equator). Thus, it is not perfectly balanced on its 23.5-degree tilted axis; as a result, the axis shifts ever so slightly, resembling a wobble. Imagine a spinning top (which is not perfectly spherical either). Its speed is such that as the top is spinning, you can see that the balance is not perfect; the wobble in the top's rotation is visible. For the earth, this wobble is a slow process, taking approximately 26,000 years to complete one circle (1 degree difference every 71.5 years). This is termed the precession of the equinoxes and was discovered by the Greek astronomer Hipparchus in approximately 125 BCE, well after the Babylonians had created the twelve-constellation zodiac. Although the difference was small at the time, the stars had been observed long enough for astronomers to notice it. One example is that although the North Pole is currently aligned with Polaris, that was not true 3,000 years ago, and by 14,000 CE, the North Star will be Vega.

## TROPICAL VERSUS SIDEREAL

Adding to the complexities is the fact that astrologers use two different systems: tropical and sidereal. Each has a different perspective on the starting point from which calculations, such as the signs of the zodiac, are based. The English and metric measurement systems are a good analogy. Both are used to measure the same things, and one can be converted to the other, but they will never exactly match because the base systems are different.

The sidereal system is the older of the two and uses the location of the sun relative to the stars as the clock by which the passage of time is measured.[7] In this system, the stars are considered fixed; thus, 0-degrees Aries is calculated as being in the same place in the sky as it was when the Babylonians first described the stars. This system is most common in astrology outside of Europe and the United States.

The tropical system views the sun's position as central to its calculations, with the position of the sun relative to the earth's horizon being the clock.[8] These changes result in the seasons, which are bounded by the solstices and equinoxes. In this system's zodiac, the spring equinox of the Northern Hemisphere is designated 0-degrees Aries, and the other signs are designated at 30-degree increments around

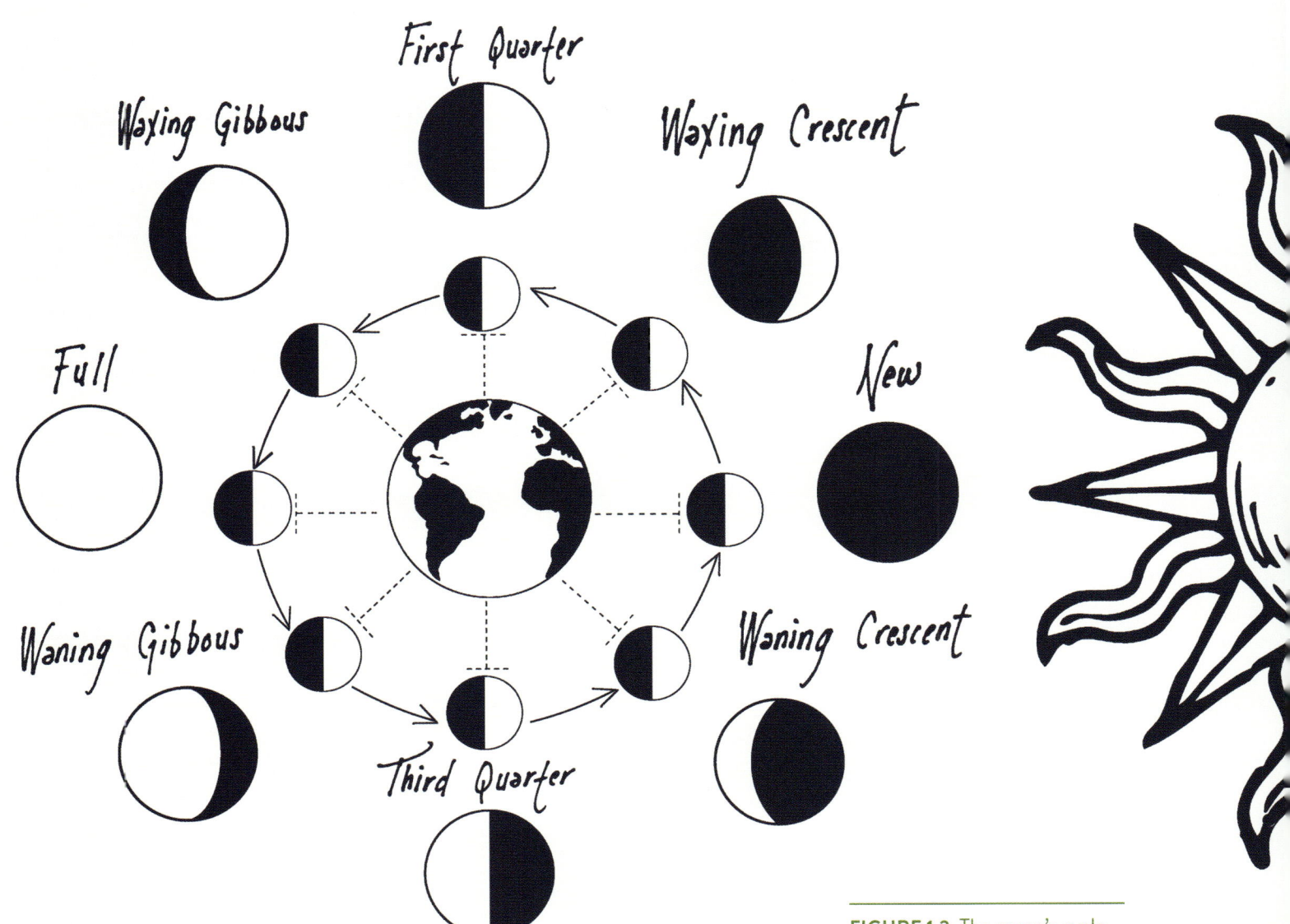

**FIGURE 1.2.** The moon's cycle as it orbits the earth. The inner ring shows the approximately twenty-eight-day cycle. The outer ring shows the moon as it appears from earth. *Illustration by Heather Dent.*

that. Because the tropical system does not rely on the notion that the stars are fixed, and because it uses the equinox as the starting point, it incorporates the precession of the equinoxes. Most Western astrologers use the tropical zodiac system.

So how much do the two systems differ? When the two zodiacs are compared side by side—or, for easier visualization, overlaid like two wheels—the difference affects around 23 of the 30 degrees within each sign. Although there are some hours during which both systems have the earth in the same moon sign, for most of the hours they differ.[9] As time passes, that difference increases with the precession of the equinoxes.

Neither the tropical nor the sidereal zodiac should be confused with the astronomical or constellational zodiac, which accounts for differences in the size of the constellations (larger ones being assigned larger slices of the pie) and encompasses constellations in addition to the twelve included in the astrological zodiacs. Ophiucus is the most commonly recognized addition to the constellational zodiac, but there may be others.[10] Some of these features have been incorporated into a relatively new system termed astronomical, constellational, or true sidereal astrology. In this system, the number of degrees assigned to each constellation varies greatly, from 6.5 to 44.

## THE MOON CYCLE: PHASES AND QUARTERS

The moon orbits the earth, with a complete cycle taking twenty-eight days (more or less).[11] The visible part of the moon—that is, the part that faces the earth (the "near side")—remains the same during its revolution.[12] The moon's backdrop, or location in the sky relative to the earth, changes as it orbits, and the moon's orientation to the sun changes (as shown in figure 1.1). The moon's orientation to the sun dictates how much of the moon is visible (or "lit") in the night sky. Thus, from a given point on earth, the moon looks a bit different during each day of its twenty-eight-day orbit. This visible change is known as the phases of the moon.

In addition to the specific phases of the moon, this cycle is divided into quarters. The first quarter is the week between the new moon and the first quarter moon (top right quadrant of figure 1.2). During this time, the visible portion of the moon (outer ring of figure 1.2) is increasing (waxing). The second quarter includes the week between the first quarter moon and the full moon (top left quadrant of figure 1.2). During this quarter, the moon is still waxing. The first and second quarters together (top half of the figure) are often termed the light or growing moon. The week between the full moon and the last quarter moon (bottom left quadrant of figure 1.2) is termed the third quarter. During this time, the visible portion of the moon is decreasing (waning). Finally, the fourth quarter encompasses the time from the last quarter moon to the new moon (bottom right quadrant of figure 1.2). The third and fourth quarters together (bottom half of the figure) are often termed the dark moon, and the fourth quarter is sometimes called the old moon.

## LUNAR DETAILS

The moon's orbit around the earth is slightly tilted (–5 degrees) in comparison to the earth's orbit around the sun. If the two were aligned, there would be a lunar eclipse every month at the full moon and a solar eclipse every month at the new moon. Instead, each type of eclipse occurs only twice a year, when the moon's long shadow lines up with the earth for solar eclipses, and when the earth's long shadow lines up with the moon for lunar eclipses. Understanding this cycle was important for

Jane Post's moon signs calendar.

early sky watchers, as eclipses were astounding events and were not viewed as favorable phenomena.

The shape of the moon's orbit is elliptical (rather than circular), meaning it is closer to the earth at certain times (perigee) and farther away at other times (apogee). Many believe the moon's influences are stronger when it is at perigee, and some almanacs include this information. Its elliptical shape also means that the distance covered by the moon's orbit varies between 11 and 15 degrees per day.[13] One additional complication is that the period from one new moon to the next new moon (a synodic month) is not the same as one orbit of the moon around the earth (a sidereal month). The synodic month is actually longer—that is, the moon has to go a bit further than 365 degrees to achieve the position where its far side is illuminated (new moon) because during that same period, the earth has moved along its own orbit. The sidereal month is 27.3 days, while the synodic month is 29.5 days.

And of course, in addition to the moon's interactions with the sun and the earth, interactions are occurring with other planets. Just as astrologers assigned the zodiac constellations different characteristics, they did the same with the planets. During certain periods, because of the earth's orientation relative to other objects, planets appear to be moving in reverse (or backward) through the zodiac, which is termed retrograde. This is simply an illusion from the perspective of the earth, but many people believe that certain influences are common during periods of retrograde (especially when Mercury is in retrograde).[14] The moon has planetary conjunctions as well, when, from the viewpoint of those on earth, the two are in alignment or appear to overlap. Finally, there are lunar nodes—the two points during the moon's orbit when it intersects with the sun's ecliptic. These two points, which are opposite each other along the moon's orbit, define periods in the moon's cycle when it appears to be either in front of or above the earth (ascending node) or behind or below the earth (descending node). When the moon is in the ascending node, it is between the earth and the sun, whereas in the descending node, the earth is closer to the sun.[15] Some calendars denote this as the period when the moon appears above the equator, crossing the equator, or below the equator.

## LUNAR INFLUENCES

Certain natural cycles on earth are clearly influenced by the moon. Tides are the most common example. As the moon orbits the earth, the portion of the earth closest to the moon experiences the strongest gravitational pull. This results in a bulge in the areas nearest the moon and directly opposite it. Any given point on earth located in one of those bulges (during the earth's twenty-four-hour daily rotation) experiences high tide. Low tide occurs when an area is located directly between the two bulges of high tide. Water is greatly influenced by the tidal force, so the larger the body of water, the more pronounced the effect.

The gravitational pull of the sun also has an impact on tides. Spring tides occur when the sun, earth, and moon are all aligned—that is, at full and new moon each month—causing the greatest gravitational pull on the oceans. Neap tides occur during the first and third quarter moons, when the sun's gravitational pull is minimized. Other factors, such as the distance between the earth and the moon (which varies, depending on the moon's position in its elliptical orbit), influence the extent to which the tidal force is felt on earth—that is, how high or low the tide is.

A commonly cited nonscientific example of the lunar influence is the fact that the moon's cycle is the same length as the average menstrual cycle. To some, this is a clear indication that the moon affects all living beings. There is quite a bit of scholarly research on reproductive health and its relation to the moon, as well as a multitude of other anecdotes relating to human behavior and the moon's cycle.[16]

In *Planetary Planting,* Louise Riotte links the moon's quarters and phases with water interactions in the soil and plants: "Moisture, to the newly planted seed, is all-important. I believe that the full moon, which affects all the water on the earth, causes soil moisture to rise closer to the earth's surface, where the newly planted crops can take full advantage of it. And this, to my thinking, is why consideration of the correct *phase* of the moon is so important to the success of the planting or transplanting of seeds or plants."[17]

Many believe that just as the moon causes tides, it also influences anything that contains moisture, including seeds (and the plants that grow from them). It can also affect the moisture in the soil, being pulled into and away from it (like the tides), but this effect is limited because the soil doesn't hold large quantities of water. This line of thinking pairs well with the phases of the moon, although it gets blurrier when the zodiacal signs are added to the mix.

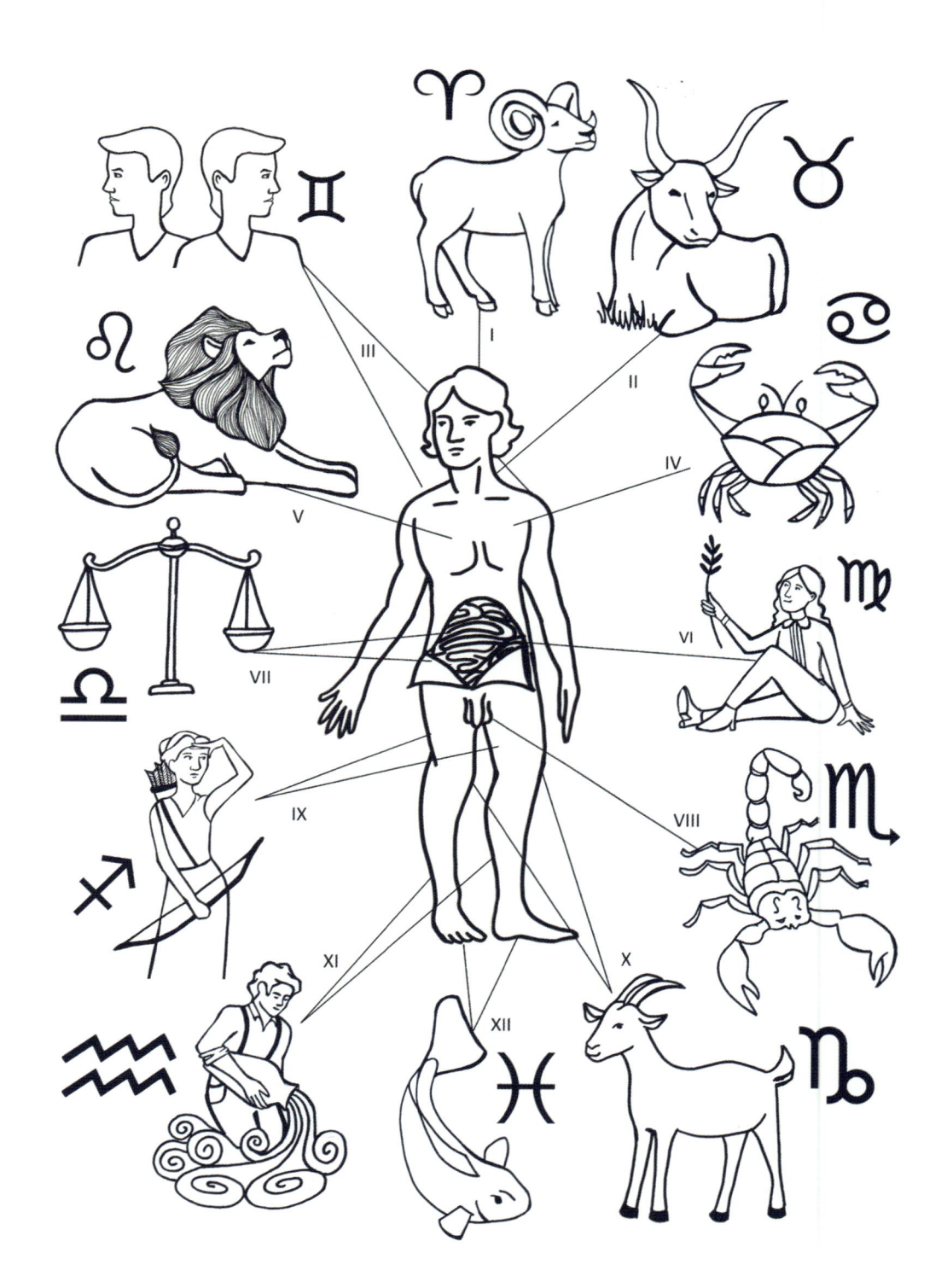

**FIGURE 1.3.** The "almanac man" or "man of signs" has been used for centuries to depict the twelve zodiac signs and their corresponding body parts. Roman numerals indicate the order of the signs in the moon's cycle. *Illustration by Heather Dent.*

## THE ALMANAC MAN

It is not entirely clear when the "almanac man" or "zodiac man" or "man of signs" came into being. The Greeks are typically credited with assigning each of the zodiacal constellations to a body part (figure 1.3), as these astrologers believed each constellation had influence over a certain part of the body. Depictions of this idea abound from various parts of the world along the timeline of human civilization. Some of the earliest records are from the Hellenistic period, although cuneiform records may predate these.[18] The body part associations (table 1.1) have remained consistent over time.

These ideas form the basis of medical astrology or astrological medicine. Among the people interviewed for this project, the vast majority referred to the zodiac signs by the body part names rather than the constellation names. All almanacs and many calendars include a version of the almanac man, and many calendars use the body part names for the days. Thus, the almanac man remains an important part of the custom of planting by the signs, even thousands of years after his inception.

TABLE 1.1. Signs of the Zodiac, Associated Body Parts, and Symbols

| SIGN | BODY PART | SYMBOL |
| --- | --- | --- |
| Aries | Head | Ram |
| Taurus | Neck | Bull |
| Gemini | Arms | Twins |
| Cancer | Breast | Crab |
| Leo | Heart | Lion |
| Virgo | Bowels | Virgin |
| Libra | Kidneys/Reins | Balance |
| Scorpio | Loins/Secrets | Scorpion |
| Sagittarius | Thighs | Bowman/archer |
| Capricorn | Knees | Goat |
| Aquarius | Legs | Waterman |
| Pisces | Feet | Fishes |

## PLANTING BY THE SIGNS

Armed with quite a bit of background information, we can now turn to the practice of planting by the signs. Specific details regarding what to do and when to do it are provided in later chapters, but planning those activities based on the moon's phase and sign is what "planting by the signs" refers to.

## Religious Links

The changing sky has been the ruling calendar since *Homo sapiens* first looked up. The fact that the stars, moon, and planets are called "heavenly bodies" is clear evidence of a link with Christianity. But other religious traditions have been born out of or arisen alongside those early astrological and astronomical observations. The links are so numerous that one wonders whether there is any ancient religion that did not rely on changes in the sky for guidance. Although some parts of astrology would be abandoned as religious thought took precedence, it is not surprising that some elements, including those more clearly tied to astronomy, remained.

In the Christian tradition, as in many others, religious holidays are set according to the celestial positionings.[19] These Christian holidays come up frequently among those who plant by the signs, especially Good Friday and ember days (revisited in later chapters). Reference to the seasons, the sun, and the moon's cycle abound in the Bible. The most commonly mentioned Bible verse by those interviewed was Ecclesiastes 3:1: "To every thing there is a season, and a time to every purpose under the heaven" (King James Version). For many, these references provide a solid religious grounding that sanctions planting by the signs.[20] There are certainly religious connections to this practice outside of the Christian tradition, given how widely it is practiced in the world, but discussion of these links is beyond the scope of this book.

## Doctrine of Signatures

Many are familiar with the doctrine of signatures as it relates to herbal medicine. This idea dates back at least 2,000 years to the Greeks. However, like so many beliefs based on the moon signs, it developed independently throughout many different cultures, making it impossible to determine its exact roots. The doctrine's premise is that the shape of a plant or a plant part is linked to its potential use in medicine. Like the other beliefs discussed, the philosophical underpinning is that divine beings want to help humans understand the natural world and therefore provide clues. Numerous common and Latin names of plants reflect this. One example is the genus *Hepatica* (meaning "of the liver"), made up of several species of common spring wildflowers that bloom throughout Appalachia. The leaves of the plant known as either liverwort or liv-

erleaf have three lobes, resembling the human liver.[21] This plant has been used to treat liver ailments dating back to the Greeks, who called it *hepar,* meaning "liver."[22]

Some believe in a similar connection between plants and the moon signs. They believe a plant's growth can be influenced in ways that reflect the sign it was planted under. One person I spoke to explained that you wouldn't want to plant anything in the Arms/Twins sign (Gemini) because the plant would develop two (or twin) flowers, and both would bear overly small fruit. The reasoning was that, like twin babies, both would make demands on the mother, and neither would reach its full potential. A different interpretation I heard was that if you planted in the Arms sign you would harvest twice as much. Others I spoke to described potatoes planted in the Feet sign (Pisces) developing knobs or little toes (some say the same about carrots).[23] Another explained that beans planted in the Feet sign bloomed first and grew beans at the base of the plant, whereas those planted in the Head sign bloomed and grew beans up top.[24] A common saying is that beans planted in the Arms will grow as long as your arm. One online comment offered this advice about potatoes: planted in the Head, they have too many eyes; for rounder boiling potatoes, plant in the Breast, and for long baking potatoes, plant in the Arms.[25]

# The Followers

## GARY AND GOLDIE EASTON, GALLATIN COUNTY

Both her parents and my parents agreed on the same thing. There were certain days that you just didn't plant tobacco and that carried over... So, we held on to that... Maybe not a whole lot of scientific proof, but it's traditions that's carried down from grandparents to parents to children.

GARY EASTON

GARY AND GOLDIE EASTON BOTH GREW UP IN Gallatin County when it was covered with tobacco farms. Although tobacco and farming are no longer the leading economic drivers in this northern Kentucky county, the Eastons continue the traditions of their parents and try to follow the signs on their 13.5-acre property. As Gary explains, "Even now, we're not involved in tobacco at all and haven't been for years, but that carried over into our lives. . . . We do plant gardens and flowers. We trim fruit trees by the signs of the moon and the signs of the zodiac. . . . So, it's been an important part of our background growing up and it still is today."

Goldie's clearest childhood memories are of her father, Sleet Maxwell. "My father was a self-taught veterinarian . . . he helped people in several of the counties there. And he would go to their farms and he would deliver their baby calves or whatever and he would castrate their hogs. But he always did that part of it by the signs." Later, Gary would go along to help those who needed it, sometimes at 3:00 a.m. (or whenever the call came). Gary's job was to hand Sleet the appropriate tools.

When the couple talks about their home, they express a humble pride for what they have accomplished. Gary explains, "Right after we got married we had the

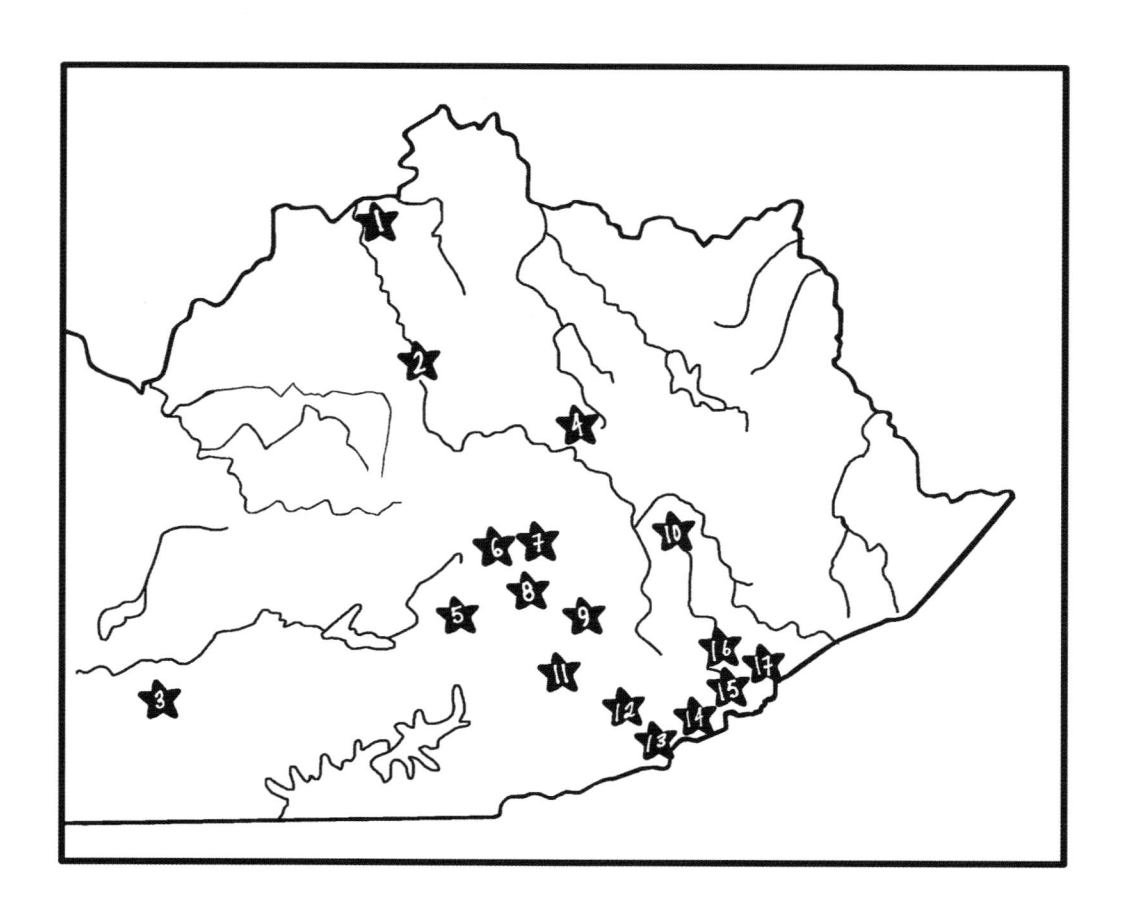

1. Gary & Goldie Easton
2. Phil Case
3. Joe Trigg
4. Julie Maruskin
5. Jess Clarkson Jr. & Bobby Clarkson
6. Bill Best
7. Jane Post
8. Susana Lein
9. Frank Jenkins
10. Clyde Charles
11. Mary Overbey
12. Anita Tolliver & Nobe Baker
13. Myrtle Turner, Abby Walker & Sarah Epperson
14. Walden Whitehead
15. Hella Shepherd
16. Hebbie Cook
17. Glenn Brown

thought of living on a piece of property that we could support ourselves, you know, self-sustaining. And although we didn't get quite that far, I think we come pretty close. We could probably live on our property for quite a while without any assistance from anyone." The couple has three children, and their fold has increased with the blessings of seven grandchildren. When I met with Gary and Goldie on the Berea College campus, they came bearing not only garden goods to be photographed (as requested) but also gifts to share, including honey and apple butter. They spoke fondly of their grandchildren's visits, which include going down into the cellar to "shop for a while." "They'll come out with quarts of green beans, quarts of tomatoes, and always, *always,* pickled beets because all the grandchildren love pickled beets."

In addition to following the traditions of their parents they learned growing up, the couple consults *The Old Farmer's Almanac* and a weekly column in the *Gallatin County News* called "Planting by the Signs," written by Phil Case. Gary sees the presence of this column as clear evidence that many in the community are still interested in traditional knowledge, even if they don't farm like they used to. "I don't believe the article in the county paper would continue to exist . . . if no one was reading it. You know, they probably wouldn't publish it. So, I think that community is still looking to the old ways."

Goldie keeps detailed records of their gardening activities, and the couple can recall with clarity examples of when the signs were right for planting or harvest-

**ABOVE, LEFT:** Goldie and Gary Easton.

**ABOVE, RIGHT:** Goldie holding a photo of her father, Sleet Maxwell.

ing and when they weren't. In 2014 the signs were right for planting sweet potatoes, and the Eastons harvested a bumper crop that year, including one that weighed nine pounds four ounces (earning it a photo and caption in the county newspaper). Their best-producing hill resulted in twenty-six pounds of sweet potatoes. They know how many pints of blueberries they froze in June (45) and how many quarts of green beans they got one year when they were especially abundant (110).

Aside from planting by the signs, the Eastons consult the signs when scheduling medical procedures, moving gravel, and putting in fence posts, among other things. Gary recalls pruning a fruit tree in the fall when the sign was in the Heart, and the tree didn't make it to the following spring. "I know some people would say, well, it probably got diseased and died. Well, it could have. But I know that I was pruning at the wrong time, so that was enough lesson for me." Goldie tries to avoid planting on ember days in June, but sometimes she just can't. She recalls, "You didn't want to be out in the field on an ember day because it just seemed so much hotter." Goldie also consulted the almanac when it was time to wean her babies, and she now passes on that information as her grandchildren are weaned. For the Eastons, both family tradition and personal experience compel them to plant by the signs and to share the results with anyone who asks.

## PHIL CASE, FRANKLIN COUNTY

*I get kind of excited about this because anything that makes something that's as labor-intensive as gardening is anyway, if you could do anything to help, why wouldn't you?*

When it comes to experts on planting by the signs, it doesn't take much asking around to hear the name Phil Case mentioned time and again. I first learned about him from my husband's aunt, who had seen him on Kentucky Educational Television (KET). I heard his name again when I interviewed the Eastons, who showed me his newspaper column. And when I asked Sarah Epperson what calendar she uses, she explained that she follows a Twitter account on planting by the signs (which Mr. Case administers). When I spoke with Phil, he easily switched between the zodiac names and the body part names, as only someone who is well versed and knows it all by heart can do.

Phil learned about planting by the signs from a neighbor of his, Buford Van Meter, who had a much better-looking garden than his own. Phil explains, "I was a hotshot twenty-two-year-old kid right out of Transylvania [University], you know. I've come to [the] little town [of] Frankfort to show them how life outta be lived. I come here, and I find this guy that can garden, that really gardens well." When Phil inquired why that might be, his neighbor was happy to begin the education process, saying, "'Well, I'll tell you: I plant by the phases of the moon, signs of the zodiac.'"

"So I, of course, had to prove it to myself, so I did that on this plot . . . probably in the summer of 1970 or so. And the crop was just unbelievable. The change was just simply by picking the date you planted on. And what sign the zodiac was in at that time." Phil became a believer that year, and he continued to follow the lessons he learned from Mr. Van Meter, whether he was tending a large garden plot or only a few raised beds. He then switched roles and became a teacher on the topic when he took a job writing for the *State Journal* newspaper in around 1977, creating a column that explained how to plant by the signs. He informed readers what conditions would be present the following week and what activities were favored (or discouraged).

In the late 1990s he supplemented his column with the details of an experiment he carried out. "We did what we called 'The Great Tomato Project' because I wanted to prove to people (they were naysayers and nonbelievers, and there are plenty) that this would work." He enlisted the help of a local nurseryman and instructed him to plant tomatoes at different times, based on different combinations of phases of the moon and signs of the zodiac. He explains, "You have two aspects of this, the phases of the moon—light moon or dark moon—and then the signs of the zodiac." For aboveground plants, a light moon is best, and the best signs can be remembered with the mnemonic "Signs Plant Thick Crops," for Scorpio, Pisces, Taurus, and Cancer. For The Great Tomato Project, Phil had the nurs-

Phil Case.

eryman plant during the best signs and then told him, for "the next one . . . I want you to do a good sign but the dark moon. Then I want you to do the light moon but a bad sign."[1]

Phil Case has been a dedicated teacher, and like all good teachers, his influence is impossible to quantify. Through his newspaper columns, he has shared the knowledge passed on to him verbally with many readers. He now has a Facebook page and a Twitter feed and is followed by many people across the country and even internationally. (At last look, his Facebook page had 7,500 followers.) And you might think that after thirty-five years of spreading the word, he would be ready for a break or might be thinking of throwing in the towel. But, as he explains, his Gemini nature means he has always had two (or more) jobs—being a minister and being a writer. "I love talking about it. I love writing about it. I love doing it."

Phil shares the almanac he uses, with the ember days marked so he doesn't miss them.

## JOE TRIGG, BARREN COUNTY

*Normally, I would have to go and ask one of the older farmers . . . is now a good time? Because you know a lot of this [is] just folklore stuff and things that they just know. And it's that group that's really eighty and above now, and they're a dyin' breed, and that's a lost art.*

Joe Trigg has been involved in farming all his life, and in many more ways than most. He has grown pretty much everything that can be grown here, and he's sold to just about all the markets that exist. He has had a "pay what you can" farm stand and has sold at the farmers' market. He has grown and sold tomatoes to a large grocery chain and raised lettuce for a farm-to-school program at the rate of 1,000 heads per week. His

Squash and tomatoes growing in the greenhouse.

grounded sense of what works well and what doesn't comes from an interesting array of personal experiences, including his travels around the globe while serving in the US Air Force for twenty-eight years. Upon his retirement in 2007 he returned to Kentucky, and when we met, he was in the midst of a campaign for agriculture commissioner.

Joe moves seamlessly from discussions about growing peppers or strawberries in a greenhouse, to feeding beef cattle in rainy weather, to the many ways the agricultural system in Kentucky and the rest of the nation is broken and could learn from methods used in other parts of the world. He is well versed in the practices touted by the Cooperative Extension Service and knows from his own experience and expertise that those practices tend to benefit some and exclude others. Overall, Joe displays a deep respect for older farmers and their learned knowledge, while keeping an eye toward what's next for farming and how Kentucky can make positive changes.

Joe is a tinkerer and is constantly thinking about new and more efficient ways of doing things. With a goal of self-sufficiency and sustainability, he has used integrated pest management and has tried aquaculture production in his greenhouses. As Kentucky moves forward, he believes hemp will become an important part of the agricultural economy. His greenhouse is filled with plants growing in different kinds of "containers," including plastic bags managed using "fertigation," and he has developed his own companion planting scheme based on experience. When he saw the price tag on a commercially available seeder, he designed his own seeder for transplant flats (utilizing an old vacuum and a custom-made screening plate). Joe's business is a family affair, with his brother and cousins helping when they can.

Joe recalls that, as a boy, he always had a vegetable garden to help feed his family and neighbors. He also remembers that anyone looking for work would go to Ideal Hardware, where farmers would come to hire help for the day. Tobacco was in its heyday at the time, and there was plenty of good (but hard) work to be had. Many of Joe's ideas about how to do things today are rooted in his experience with tobacco. He now talks about a quota system for hemp, and much of the equipment and supplies he has repurposed got their start in tobacco.

When it comes to the signs, Joe first heard older folks passing the time at the hardware store saying things like, "The signs ain't right." Now he laments that he didn't pay attention to their conversations. Only when he got older and started traveling the globe did he notice that many different places used a system of planting based on the moon signs. The practice is much more prevalent in other parts of the world, which Joe attributes to multiple variables. One is that other regions have a much longer agricultural history than the United States. Another is that other countries don't have the vast resources we do, so there is more incentive to get things right. "We're Americans. We just say, 'No, we don't have to do that.' We can plow and plant, we got enough land [so] if it don't work we'll plow another hundred acres and plant, ya know?"

By the time he returned home to Kentucky and started his agricultural operation, Joe had become a quick learner. When he ramped up to sell tomatoes to a grocery chain, he got involved with Red River Research out of Louisiana State University. Folks there told him if he didn't plant at a certain time, the seeds would rot. He also observed that when he started growing lettuce and planted seeds on a regular weekly schedule, sometimes the seeds wouldn't germinate, but other times they would germinate in two days. He now goes by a calendar he gets at his local farm supply store (but it's available at all the old insurance companies and seed companies, so long as you get there early, before they're gone) and cross-references that with a "cheat sheet" he created from the back page of a *Gardening by the Moon* calendar.[2] His cheat sheet is numbered 1 to 8 in the following order from best to worst signs for planting: Cancer, Scorpio, Pisces, Taurus, Virgo, Capricorn, Libra, and Aries. (The ones not listed should be avoided altogether.) About his system, Joe says, "To me this is good. My scientific application of something that's unexplainable."

## JULIE ANN NARVELL MARUSKIN, CLARK COUNTY

Ya know, so I can tell people, and I do tell our patrons, that I personally colloquially really can't tell that much difference. But I like Louise Riotte, the woman who wrote *Planetary Planting*. I'm a Libra like she was, so I do plant all my flowers in Libra. Because it's fun, and it's about me. And I have great luck with my flowers.

If you want to talk to Julie Maruskin about the signs, you must first understand some things about her mother: Sonya Mae Wilson Narvell was sending her children to school with homemade brown bread when it was not cool to do so. She "was a hard-core southern Baptist hippie chick" who taught yoga in the 1960s and 1970s, but as she explained to Julie and her sister, they were just practicing the poses (not the religion) of yoga. It was Sonya's family that kept and passed down the tradition of planting by the signs, which, as Julie explains, her mother claims is a scientifically proven method.

Julie is not entirely sure when she first heard about the signs from her mother, but she guesses she was about four years old, when she was put in charge of planting Black Seeded Simpson lettuce and strawberry popcorn in the family garden. She vividly recalls her mother's own story from childhood: Mae (as Sonya was called back then), "being stubborn like all the women in the family," decided it was time to plant the beans she had been given responsibility over. Mae's mother (Julie's grandmother) told her it wasn't the right time to plant beans, but she did so anyway. All the beans Mae planted "blossomed to beat the band," then dropped their blooms and produced very few beans. Meanwhile, Mae's mother had also planted beans— under the correct sign, of course—and they were loaded with beans. Thus, definitive proof was provided at a very early age for Julie's mother, and three generations of women were imprinted.

Julie works at the Clark County library, and since 2000 she has helped run workshops on various aspects of gardening. In 2005 these workshops became mobile, being offered at various libraries throughout the state. The goal was to distribute heirloom seeds and teach people how to grow them. In the process, Julie and others involved in the workshops were able to find seed varieties that had been "lost" to participants' families. Julie became the curator of some varieties that she still keeps today, long after those who gifted her the seeds have passed. These workshops educated an incredible number of people in Kentucky well before the current hype around local food and seed saving.

Like any good seed saver, Julie knows where each of her treasures came from and when they date to. She grows a bean she calls Dilman's Bush Cut-short that came from the grandmother of a friend from Tennessee. And she grows a Peter Pepper ("it's anatomically correct," she laughs), a variety that goes back to the mid-1800s. In addition to reviving and saving old seeds obtained from others, Julie has done some selective breeding of her own. She developed Maruskin's Andes, a paste tomato selected from an Andes variety that is at least 250 years old. She explains, "We've selected it so that it's bigger and thinner skinned and it holds up well. This one holds up really well to blight; it's used to Kentucky's weird blight patterns."

Julie Maruskin.

The Peter Pepper Julie saves seeds from.

As the workshop series grew, Julie created a calendar as a fundraiser for the library that highlights what should be done on each day of the year. It is packed full of information about sources for heirloom seeds, monthly gardening tips, recipes, and, of course, the moon phase and zodiac sign for each day. Julie has done extensive research on the different almanacs and calendars and has become something of an expert on them. "I started collecting almanacs just because I was interested in how the calculations worked and the differences that we see from country to country, Northern Hemisphere and Southern Hemisphere, sidereal and tropical. And it's very complex and kinda hinky around the periphery of it, so some of it is based in mathematical calculations, some of it is based in folklore. I find that really attractive in a weird way."

Julie's garden teems with beans, tomatoes, peppers, greens, and daylilies. She tries her best to follow the signs because, she says, "I feel like if I'm producing a garden moon sign calendar then I at least ought to walk the walk." Julie has amazing luck with flowers, which she *always* plants in first or second quarter Libra. She herself is a Libra (sun sign), which may contribute to her success. According to her family's tradition, your sun zodiacal sign says something about you and your personality (which many believe to be true), but during the moon sign under which you were born, that sign's favorable activities can be amplified. "You can double the effects," Julie says. As an example, she is a third quarter Sagittarius (moon sign), which is said to favor digging. "So, if I'm out in my yard and it's third quarter Sagittarius, I should be able to double dig a trench for sweet peas in no time flat. My mother is a fourth quarter Sagittarius, and anything that woman cleans stays clean, because that's a sign where you would go out and raze things to the ground and it would be done." And Julie's sister, a second quarter Cancer (the most fruitful of all the signs), "can grow anything she touches."

# JESS CLARKSON JR. AND BOBBY CLARKSON, LINCOLN COUNTY

*Well, of course I've heard of them [the moon signs] all my life; my wife, he- family, and all of 'em believed in it, well, my mother and my dad too.*

JESS CLARKSON JR.

To sit and talk with Jess Clarkson Jr. is like speaking with a living history book. His father, Jess Clarkson Sr., was born in 1858, so just one generation back was the pre–Civil War era. Jess Sr. was sixty-three years old when Jess Jr. was born. "Yeah, I got some old blood in me, old genes," says Jess. At age ninety-four he can still recall his days in World War II with photo clarity. He remembers childhood days when the sun looked like the moon, filtered by dust of different colors blowing through the skies, depending on where it came from out west. He recalls tobacco more than doubling its size with the advent of fertilizers and pesticides. And he recalls hard times during the Great Depression, when many people were barely scraping by. Of that time he says, "You either farmed or starved." He calls his family blessed because they had a few chickens and a peach orchard that allowed them to live pretty well. Jess also did his fair share of clearing new ground to add to his family's farming acreage.

Bobby Clarkson (*left*) and Jess Clarkson Jr. (*right*).

Jess's grandson Bobby chimes in during our interview to brag on the elder Mr. Clarkson, who was clearing new ground for tobacco just before going off to boot camp at age sixteen or seventeen: "I told him, I said, 'You were stronger [going in] than a lot of guys after boot camp.'" Clearing ground was hard work—cutting the timber, hauling it out, plowing the ground, and then, finally, planting. While Jess was doing all that work on his own that summer, he began to dream of getting a horse, and after the war he bought himself a team of them (it cost him $340—"a lot of money at that time"). After the war he also attended Farm School, sponsored by the precursor to the Cooperative Extension Service. He was paid $90 per month to attend classes and participate in field days.

When it came to deciding when and what to plant, Jess's late wife, Gladys, was the keeper of knowledge about the signs. His parents also believed in the signs, and he followed their lead. He recalls planting beans based on blooming days and avoiding pruning or other activities on ember days. Jess and his family would consult the *Farmers' Almanac* every year. He has grown just about every type of plant and raised nearly every type of animal that can live in Kentucky, and he can still tell you with precision how to go about it. Jess can tell you all about growing, harvesting, and storing corn and tobacco with only hand tools and lots of incredibly hard work.

When asked about the signs, Jess says, "Course you had a lot of people that believed in it, and some that didn't believe in it, and they done just about as well, ya know, in a way." Of his late wife he says, "Gladys . . . she was really talented, more than I was, on some things, she was really good . . . on stuff like that." His grandson Bobby adds, "She taught me all the trees and some of the herbs and different plants in the woods . . . she knew a lot of the birds, the bugs, and she knew more about the signs." Bobby recalls a time when his grandfather's neighbors planted tobacco and it didn't come up. The neighbors attributed the failure to planting in the wrong sign.

## BILL BEST, MADISON COUNTY

As an observer of nature, what I've noticed, ya know, a force like the moon, that can create tides on earth, is naturally gonna deal with the plants. It just makes sense. It's not just old-fashioned thinking. It's being aware of the forces of nature around you.

Anyone who knows about heirloom seed saving in Appalachia knows Bill Best. He has written two books on the subject and is the creator and former director of the Sustainable Mountain Agriculture Center.[3] For decades, Bill's entire existence has been about preserving the seeds of our ancestors—those seeds that bear food worth saving. He has grown more than 1,200 different types of beans and more than 500 tomato varieties. Bill recently learned from a DNA test that he has some Cherokee blood, making his ancestral link with the beans he grows even stronger than he realized. When asked to describe a favorite meal, Bill chooses his nontough half-runner greasy beans (seasoned with fatback, ham hock, or bacon) with buttered cornbread

and diced onions and, if available, sliced tomatoes (preferably Vinson Watts variety) on top.

Bill speaks of his farming endeavors with incredible pride, so it is not a surprise that he was introduced to planting by the signs by a neighbor who grew better beans than he did. Lucy Alexander, who lived just up the road, asked Bill if she might use his greenhouse (which was under construction at the time, more than twenty years ago) to dry her shuck beans. Bill commented to Lucy that her beans always seemed to grow better than his (they even maintained some of their green color while drying), and she informed Bill that he often planted his beans in the wrong sign. For many years thereafter, he would take his calendar to Lucy and she would mark the proper time to plant beans (in the Arms/Gemini).

The next fall, as they were both spreading their beans out to dry, Bill remarked to Lucy that his beans had done better than hers that year, to which she replied, "They ought to be, you have better ground than I do." Lucy has since passed away, but the impression she made on Bill remains. He says, "To make a long story short, I believe very much in planting by the signs, but I just haven't had enough time to do it, to test it out, but I try to do it when I can." He has known many folks who pay attention to the signs not just for planting but also for castrating animals, cutting trees, and just about anything else.

**ABOVE, LEFT:** Bill Best.

**ABOVE, RIGHT:** Bill looks over his shuck beans in the same greenhouse that brought him and his neighbor Lucy together so many years ago.

# JANE POST, MADISON COUNTY

*It's almost like it [the moon] was placed there—if you believe in God, if you believe in aliens, it was placed there. . . . So that it does affect our tides, and it does affect everything.*

Jane Post.

Jane Post sees astrological connections to just about every task done in a given day. At her home, called Forest Retreats, she holds several workshops, and she makes sure to schedule them outside of a Mars aspect, as accidents are more likely to happen then. She advertises the workshops during a sign that is favorable for communication. She has noticed that even during very dry spells, there will be some rain during the fruitful water signs (Cancer is the most fruitful). She tries her best to combat pests and weeds on barren days and notes that her husband's mushroom logs bear lots of fruiting bodies during a full moon. She says it's not a bad idea to consult the stars (or *Llewellyn's Moon Sign Book*, as she does) when considering making an investment, signing papers, scheduling travel (be sure Mercury isn't in retrograde), or undergoing surgery. When talking to Jane, it's easy to get caught up in the complexity of what's going on in the heavens and to feel that many forces are at play in our daily lives. It's not only the phases of the moon (first quarter for planting annuals, second quarter for fruit-bearing plants, third quarter for root crops, and fourth quarter for controlling pests) or the zodiac signs (classified as the earth elements) that matter but also the precession of the planets and the orientation of the earth and the moon.

Although she sounds like a lifelong follower of all things astrological, Jane was a minister's daughter and moved around quite a bit during her childhood. Admittedly, she may have been drawn to the astrological lessons she read in the Foxfire books due to their off-limits nature (she proudly calls herself a rebel). It was when she moved to Pennsylvania around age fifteen that she first took up farming, growing food in the family garden. Her reading of the Foxfire books also sparked her curiosity about planting by the signs. After attending Berea College, Jane met several "old-timers" who shared everything about their practices, including planting by the signs. The 250 acres Jane and her husband, Tim, own are mostly forested hillside, with their home and garden occupying a narrow holler with limited sunlight. She grows lots of greens, tomatoes, sweet corn, potatoes, squash, and peppers, and the couple eats lots of wild foods

from their woods. She admits she didn't always have time in the past to follow the signs, but since she retired and has been able to do so, her garden has done remarkably better. Her passion on the subject is enough to make a believer of anyone.

## SUSANA LEIN, ROCKCASTLE COUNTY

There's a lot of truth to it, I believe . . . but like other spiritual things you choose to believe them and try to support processes of nature that you don't fully understand. And we never will. And part of my philosophy of permaculture is to work with those processes as much as I can.

Susana Lein practices permaculture—an integrated approach to agriculture, natural building, and more that mimics closed-loop systems like those found in nature—on her Salamander Springs Farm, a diversified subsistence and market farm in the Clear Creek Valley near Berea. Susana grew up on a small farm in Iowa in the 1960s and 1970s, when farms included both animals and vegetables. She laments that

Susana Lein.

such a landscape no longer exists in that region, having been swallowed up by industrial monoculture farms. It wasn't until Susana moved to Guatemala in the 1990s that she heard of the connections between farming practices and the moon. When cutting some carrizo (a plant similar to bamboo) to repair her chicken fencing, Susana was informed by her Mayan neighbors that she was cutting it in the wrong sign. She didn't think much of it until she saw that the newly cut stalks were rotting in the ground much faster than the carrizo already in the fence, which she had cut years earlier with a Mayan farmer. Susana brought this and many other lessons with her when she moved to Kentucky in 1999.

After purchasing a mostly forested property in the Appalachian foothills, she cleared about five acres of overgrown ridgetop meadow and began to build her soil intensively and follow permaculture practices on her land. She doesn't till and raises an astonishing number of crops, including numerous vegetables as well as staples such as beans and corn. She also grows many different fruits, berries, nuts, herbs, flowers, forest foods, and medicinals. Susana practices the "three sisters" method of intercropping (beans, corn, and squash), which she learned from the Pokomchí people in Guatemala. She tries her best to follow the *Stella Natura* biodynamic calendar.[4] She first heard about Kentuckians planting by the moon signs from Daymon Morgan in Leslie County (a mentor who in 1999 shared a few ears of corn with her that became the parental seed stock for the Kentucky Rainbow dent corn she developed).[5] She later learned from others closer to her valley (including Jane Post and Bill Best) about what she calls "Appalachian old-timers' methods" of planting by the moon, such as planting on Good Friday (when the full moon starts) and focusing primarily on the phases of the moon.

In her farming practice, Susana has noticed that root crops are especially influenced by planting in the right sign (passage of a full moon helps pull the roots down). The biodynamic calendar she uses designates the zodiac signs as flower, leaf, fruit, or root signs, indicating which types of crops are best to work with at that time. Like other guides, it clearly spells out daily recommendations and when transitions occur, and as Susana says, "You don't have to really learn why or understand it when you go by the calendar, you just look at the calendar . . . it's all determined." It also designates the perigee (the point at which the moon is closest to the earth),

Salamander Springs Farm is off the grid and uses permaculture practices such as terracing and the incorporation of poultry.

Susana's stand is a popular spot at the Berea farmers' market, bursting with seasonal offerings as well as her staples. (Photo from https://salamandersprin gs.wixsite.com/farm)

at which time there are blackout periods and nothing should be done. As a market gardener, Susana can't always follow the calendar, but she says, "There is definitely power that comes from our cosmic field that we aren't as in tune with."

## FRANK JENKINS, JACKSON COUNTY

With the moon signs, you really prepare for whatever you're gonna be doing because you know that time is coming up. For me, the moon signs are always encouragement to prepare for whatever you're going to accomplish. . . . So if you plan your life by doing things by the signs, then you are planning for success.

Frank Jenkins.

Frank Jenkins calls himself a traditional skills practitioner. Others might say he is an old-timey jack-of-all-trades. He grew up in Jefferson County (near Louisville) when there were still farms and rural areas there. He recalls a dairy farm just across the road from his house on a dead-end street, and he spent time exploring old fields that were transforming into woods on property owned by the Kentucky Military Institute. His childhood also included frequent visits with friends and neighbors of his grandmother, who lived and farmed in Estill County. Since that time, Frank has done all sorts of things to honor the traditional ways. He splits his time between two properties and picks up work demonstrating, teaching, and using his traditional skills when he can.

The first time I met Frank he was building a stone structure for an urban farm I was touring with one of my classes. Then we chatted at a Pine Mountain Settlement School event, where I was recruiting folks to interview for this project. After we had talked for a while, it became apparent that although he spoke more highly of other folks he had learned from, Frank himself knew quite a lot about the signs, especially with regard to animal husbandry. And in every encounter, it seemed some new skill became evident in his stories. In addition to dry stone masonry, Frank has had experience raising and butchering livestock (including raising a dairy cow on heritage fodder beets he grew himself and milking her by hand), farming and logging with horses, and curing and smoking meat. Some of his favorite meals are one-pot recipes he cooks on a wood-burning stove. He remembers a host of old sayings he has picked up along the way, such as "Sow your turnips in July and you'll have turnips wet or dry" and "Plant your garlic on the shortest day of the year and harvest it on the longest day of the year."

Into his teenage years, Frank started to show more interest in farming and gardening and paid more attention to the old people who were still planting by the signs. He recalls that his grandfather planted his potatoes in the dark of the moon, but beyond that, Frank mostly did what others told him. He says, "The major regret is I didn't really pay attention to when things were being done except the old people said it was time to. The people that lived by 'em [the signs] said, 'Well, it's time to plant your whatever.' . . . So I didn't really pay that much attention to actually the signs themselves. I didn't have to retain that knowledge because the old folks had it." Today he uses the chart from *The Old Farmer's Almanac.*

Those who don't follow the signs for planting are said to "plant in the ground," a phrase I heard quite a few times during interviews and one that is clearly understood by many. Frank is more familiar with the parallel term for castrating animals when conditions are less than favorable (mostly due to the weather). At those times, folks say, "The sign's in the knife, let's go cut them pigs." He has talked to the people who work at the local butcher shop, and although they don't follow the signs, they do wonder whether that might be the reason certain days don't go well for slaughtering.

Because he is a jack-of-all-trades, Frank also knows about the moon signs in relation to construction activities and general farmwork. For example, putting on shake shingles should be done in the dark of the moon. From his masonry work he knows, "If we're putting down stepping-stones, you want to put them down in the light of the moon so they'll stay on top of the ground. And if you're pouring a footer or putting something in the ground, like a fence post, then you do that in the dark of the moon." Setting fence posts by the signs is a common practice Frank has heard about many times. It is said that if post holes are dug in the wrong sign, there will be a lot of dirt left over, but if you do it at the right time, you'll need more dirt because it packs down so much better.

When Frank talks, it is easy to hear that he pines for the old ways. He has, after all, spent his life trying to preserve them. He laments that technological advances come at the cost of the traditional skills and knowledge we relied on when we were more connected to the earth. One example is salt-curing meat. Frank knows there is a good sign for killing and butchering a hog to get a nice full ham, whereas in other signs the meat shrinks and doesn't cure as well. He can't remember which signs are which, though, "because nobody for the most part salts their hams anymore, and we don't scald hogs, we skin 'em. And then use a freezer." Frank reminds us that, as in many cultures, the Appalachian custom of following the signs has been transferred primarily by an oral tradition that accompanies the work being done. And as that work changes, much is lost. Frank is doing what he can to preserve those traditions while living in the modern world.

## CLYDE CHARLES, LEE COUNTY

> Well, back then . . . it was eight of us in the family, it took a whole lot to keep us going. You rendered your own lard, you ground your own meal, and you made your own molasses. And you had sweet potatoes and Irish potatoes and all your canned stuff you raised in the garden. That's how we lived. You didn't go to the store to get everything like they do today.

Clyde Charles has spent his life in Lee County, Kentucky. The youngest of six children, Clyde says his family tended "anywhere from about fifteen to twenty acres of corn, about two acres of cane, and probably an acre garden" on land they leased. He spent his childhood helping with the farmwork until he went to high school at age sixteen. By then, being the youngest, all his siblings had already gotten married and left home.

Clyde's mom, Eunice Charles, taught him about the signs. She wouldn't plant anything when it was in the Bowels, but she liked to plant in any sign below the Thighs (the Knees or the Feet were good). She would consult the *Farmers' Almanac,* and Clyde still uses a calendar he gets every year from Congleton Brothers Hardware Store in Beattyville. A lot of the corn they raised went to feed the family's five or six hogs. Clyde recalls folks paying attention to the moon when it was time to kill a hog, avoiding the new moon because the meat would puff up. Besides corn and sorghum, the Charles family raised just about everything that will grow in Kentucky: green beans, tomatoes, peas, lettuce, cabbage for kraut, and blackberries for jams and jellies. Perhaps the Charles family's signature crop, though, was the potato—both sweet and Irish.

Clyde remembers those potatoes well and continues to grow them. He says he and his siblings would make 150 hills of sweet potatoes. And he learned not to plant Irish potatoes in the new moon "because they grow on top of the ground, turn green. Then if you plant them on the old of the moon, they'll get deep, and it's a lot harder to dig. But I always plant mine on about the first quarter, any time after that." When to dig potatoes is also important, with the old of the moon being the time when any cuts will heal over. "I've got some down in the basement now to prove that one," Clyde says. "I stuck a fork plumb through some of 'em the other day down there and they ain't rotted." The potatoes are stored by burying them in a bed of straw or hay with more on top, followed by about eight inches of dirt and finally a layer of fodder to shed water.

Clyde's daughter Deborah chimes in and says, "The potatoes was always big and good. That was the main staple. If you didn't have potatoes and cornbread when I was growing up, you didn't have a meal." She admits to ignoring her father's advice about when to plant potatoes and then becoming a believer. "I wouldn't listen to him and I would plant my potatoes in a different time and I didn't have no potatoes. And he come out here and had the awfulest potatoes I ever seen. I mean they were big, and I'm left thinking I can't get nothing but marbles out of 'em." Admiration is something Clyde is accustomed to. Growing up, he said, "We had people complain, 'How do you do that? We plant our garden and we take good care of it [but] it don't grow like that.'"

Clyde Charles stands in front of his castor beans, which he grows every year to keep the groundhogs out. (Photo by Sarah Hall)

Unearthed potatoes.

# MARY OVERBEY, LAUREL COUNTY

I've heared back then when we were growing up that a lot of people would say that they'd go to bed hungry, didn't have anything to eat. But we always had plenty to eat.

Mary Overbey has lived her entire life in an area called Piney Grove in Laurel County, Kentucky. She was one of ten children who regularly helped out at home, whether it was hauling water and washing clothes on a board or working out in the garden or in the kitchen. The house she lives in now, her home for fifty-three years, is just a few "blocks" (in the country sense) from the site of the log cabin where she grew up. She speaks respectfully of her mother, who raised her and her siblings at a time when life was much different from now. Her father was a well driller and traveled throughout the county. The family raised tobacco and pretty much everything they ate. Corn was a staple and was shelled and hauled to the mill in winter to be ground into cornmeal. They grew potatoes, beans, cabbage, onions, tomatoes, peppers, watermelons, cantaloupes, squash, and pumpkins, and they raised milk cows, beef cattle, and hogs as well. Mary recalls, "We loved cornbread and milk. Had all kinds of other vegetables and meat to go with it."

Mary Overbey.

Her parents planted by the signs, with beans and potatoes being the two main crops for which the signs mattered. Her father always planted and dug potatoes during the old moon, and her mother planted beans on the Arms or Twin days. Although Mary respects traditions, here she veers from her mother's guidance. She says of beans planted on the Twin days, "They just curl up in the ground and won't come through the ground, a lot of them don't. Which the old people used to plant them in Twin days all the time, but I never have liked that." She prefers to plant her beans in the Secrets (Loins) or Breast. "Actually, the Secrets are better than the Cancer/Breast."

When I visited, Mary had quarts of beans sitting out for her granddaughter, who was also there. Mary was polite and brief in her answers. When I asked what her favorite food from her garden was, she said without hesitation, "green beans." Not one to brag about her accomplishments, Mary had to be prompted for further explanation, and it was her granddaughter who asked how much she had canned this year. The answer was 200 quarts. (Mary hadn't grown that many beans herself, although her two rows had yielded six bushels—nothing to sneeze at.) With three children of her own, four grandchildren, and nine great-grandchildren, Mary uses her canned green beans as a way to share her love and hard work with them all.

## ANITA TOLLIVER AND NOBE BAKER, HARLAN COUNTY

I don't ever remember a time that I didn't know about gardening. When I grew up, Mom and Dad always had a garden, my grandparents always had a garden. I was fortunate enough to have living great-grandparents. So, there were always gardens. I grew up realizing you just didn't run out and throw the seeds in the ground and go on. There had to be a rhyme and a reason to the way you planted things.

ANITA TOLLIVER

Anita Tolliver participated in a Foxfire project that involved learning various teaching methods from Eliot Wigginton at Berea College in the 1980s, and when I met her at an event at Pine Mountain Settlement School, she was enthusiastic about my project. However, she informed me that it was her father I needed to meet. I visited with Anita and her father, Nobe Baker, on Mr. Baker's porch along Highway 221, just a few miles from Pine Mountain Settlement School, on a warm October afternoon. Her father sat quietly as she signed the forms for the project. But when it came time for Nobe to sign, he expressed mistrust of being recorded; he didn't want to be seen as a damned hillbilly, like had happened to someone he knew. He was happy to talk and have his picture taken, but no recorder.

The memories of both Anita and her father are deep and filled with admiration for the way they and their families have done things when it comes to food. Perhaps the fact that Nobe's people are so long-lived has something to do with that. Alice Huff Lewis, or "Mamm" to Anita, was Nobe's maternal grandmother. Anita was twenty

Nobe Baker and
Anita Tolliver.

years old when she passed, so she has lots of memories of Mamm. Anita explains in a follow-up email, "[Mamm] was the granddaughter of local legend 'Ole Man John Shell,' who supposedly was the oldest man in the world. He was rumored to be 131. However, I have researched records and his death certificate says 114 . . . still not bad!" Thus, Anita has memories of learning not only from her parents and grandparents but also from her great-grandparents (Mamm and Pap). She remembers Pap plowing with his horse Pearl. And she remembers Mamm telling the story about her mother sending her to the well to pump water for some Cherokee who were passing through.

Nobe's farming history is long, but his most recent accomplishments occurred at the Detention Center in Evarts, Kentucky. There, he helped the inmates grow so much food that the state inspected the kitchen during an audit, wondering how the inmates could be fed on only $1.57 per meal. (Nobe and Anita note that when many of the men went home, their old clothes didn't fit because they had eaten so well.) Nobe rattled off the details about the crops, as only someone fully involved could: 5 tons of seed potatoes and 2 tons of potash (plus a whole lot of work, although that's not mentioned) made 28 tons of Irish potatoes, saving $9,000 alone; 2 acres of sweet corn yielded 190 gallons; and 90 rows of beans (each 450 feet long) yielded more than 5,600 gallons. He attributes his success to the methods of planting by the signs he learned from his grandmother (Anita's Mamm). She said beans could be planted in the Twins (Arms/Gemini); otherwise, plant beans in the Knees or lower. Plant in a darkening moon for roots and in a growing moon for aboveground plants. Potatoes should be planted in a full moon, beans and corn in a new moon. And definitely don't plant in the Head or the Heart.

Nobe fondly remembers his mother's pickled cucumbers, beans, and corn. The corn stayed on the cob in the brine, and he loved fishing out beans from the big barrel when he went to the smokehouse. (Nobe and Anita explain that corn and beans should be fried in lard after pickling, not boiled.) Anita's upbringing highlighted the cycles present in everything. Crops were always rotated, and the family used every part of what nature provided. Anita says her father still spreads horse manure on the fields, and she continues to use canning jars from the 1930s. "I think that's real common of a lot of mountain people. I think we have particular ways that we do things that might be a little different."

Anita has ten black thumbs (her words), so her job is not to grow the bounty of the garden but to preserve it. That takes the form of frozen beans, cooked-down tomatoes, pickled squash, and jelly. Anita's favorites are hard to pin down, but they include canned green beans straight out of the jar, a freshly boiled ear of corn with butter and salt as a midnight snack, and a fresh cucumber from the garden shared with her grandfather (he'd cut slices with his pocketknife—one for her, one for him).

Anita is retired after a long career with the Harlan County schools, and her passion for education is clear. Her eyes widen as she relates Mamm's story about the Cherokee. She explains, "We tend to think of our history, but our history is so recent, it's not like in England or even in the southwestern United States. There's stuff back there that dates into the 1600s, and there's really not here. To think that my great-grandmother pumped water for the Native Americans that were hunting is pretty . . . , ya know. And I knew her. I was in my twenties when she passed; so that brings it all . . . into a short time span." For her part, Anita continues to honor the old ways, but she has also developed some of her own methods. Instead of canning, she freezes and vacuum-seals green beans without blanching ("They really taste more like you've gone out in the garden and just picked them"). And she cooks them in a pressure cooker, but with much less fatback or lard than her mother did. She has also experimented with making lye soap, explaining how the process works and saying, "I'm fortunate that I've got the internet and all these other ways of reading." Anita's activities are informed by the past but strengthened by continual learning.

*You don't believe it? Just try it and see.*

**MYRTLE TURNER**

Myrtle Turner is the quintessential Appalachian mamaw. She's spent nearly all her life in Big Laurel in Harlan County (she was fourteen when she moved across Big Laurel Mountain from Perry County). As one of nine children, she worked with her dad in the fields as a matter of necessity. She plowed with a mule, planted and hoed corn, planted and picked beans, canned vegetables, fed and milked cows, and churned butter. Today, she also makes tonics and other herbal medicines from the plants surrounding her home. She passed on the gardening tradition to her four children and occasionally used it as a disciplinary measure. Her daughter Abby remembers that she and her siblings were forced to hoe in the garden, to which Myrtle adds, "Especially when they wanted to skip school . . . [after] working in a garden, they didn't want to [skip school] the next day."

**LEFT TO RIGHT:** Myrtle Turner, Sarah Epperson, and Abby Walker.

Though the three women strongly believe in planting by the signs, not everyone in their family does. Myrtle's father "didn't believe in the signs; he believed in planting in the ground." It was Myrtle's mother-in-law who taught her about planting and canning by the signs. Although Abby Walker has followed in her mother's footsteps and always plants by the signs, one of Myrtle's other daughters (Sarah's mother) doesn't follow the signs and says (according to Sarah) it's just an excuse to get out of the garden. When Sarah started to garden on her own, she would take a calendar to her mamaw and have her put a checkmark or an *X* on the different days.

Sarah Epperson works as a nurse at a nursing home and has heard about the practice from some of her patients. An avid learner and documentarian, she has taken lots of notes about what her patients and her mamaw have advised. She keeps detailed records of when she plants which crops and under what sign. And she has pictures to show that her mamaw's warning about not gardening or canning while menstruating should be heeded. Some years back, Sarah happened to be canning beans and tomatoes during her time of the month, so she took the precaution of wearing gloves and thought that would prevent a bad outcome. The photographs on her phone tell a different story— her tomatoes separated (the solid parts floated to the top, leaving clear water at the bottom of the jars), and her beans "sprouted in the jar and turned milky." She also follows the "Planting by the Signs" Twitter feed by Phil Case, which largely agrees with her mamaw's advice (that is not the case for some other internet sources).

Abby looks at the "almanac man" on a smartphone, while Sarah holds a calendar as comparison.

Abby Walker does her best to continue the old ways taught by her mother, but she doesn't hesitate to google something on her phone when she has a question. She has been involved in Grow Appalachia meetings and workshops at Pine Mountain Settlement School and speaks enthusiastically about learning new ways of doing things from other people. At one program she attended, the presenter showed pictures of big broccoli heads that Abby thought couldn't be real. But then she followed the method herself and beams with pride as she shares pictures of her own impressive broccoli and cauliflower (the key was planting them late for a fall garden). In addition to canning many garden items—a process she learned from her mother—she dehydrates lots of vegetables, and her mouth waters when she describes how sweet a dried tomato is.

For these three generations of women, the old ways continue, even as they learn new ways of doing things. Throughout my time with them, Myrtle's desire to pass on her knowledge came up repeatedly, whether it was related to planting by the signs or sewing upholstery (her career for more than forty years) or how to cure poison ivy overnight. As Myrtle says, "You never get too old to learn, do you?"

## WALDEN WHITEHEAD, HARLAN COUNTY

*You have to work in it. You can't just go out there and plant this and say I'm done. I mean that's seven days a week—when I get in from work, after work. And it's enjoyment. People said, "You got a green thumb." Well, I go by the signs of planting. And I work in it—all the time.*

Walden Whitehead.

Walden Whitehead's gardens are scattered throughout his yard, partly to deceive his wife into thinking he's done when he plants each one, and partly to isolate his different beans so they remain pure. When I visited him in July, the patchwork had been filled in everywhere flat enough and accessible enough to be called "yard." As we sat and chatted on his front porch, he pointed to different areas as he talked about his different crops. He had shuck beans drying in the sun and lots more still on the vine, including speckled greasies—"Not like the kind you can buy," he qualifies—and his favorite fall beans. He also had corn, tomatoes, cucumbers, zucchini, and other squash.

Talking to Walden, you get the sense that his passion and drive will keep him gardening until his last day, even though he told his daughter he won't plant a garden next year (his wife confirms he says this every year). As a devout seed collector and saver, he laments not picking up some of those unusual-looking big speckled greasy seeds he saw about a month ago. He speaks proudly of a tomato he obtained from a preacher at Kermit Creek whose grandfather had saved the seeds, making the variety more than 200 years old (Walden's wife nearly picked the biggest green one on the vine to make fried green tomatoes, but he averted this disaster, letting her know he was saving that one for seed).

Like others I interviewed, Walden speaks fondly of spending time with family in the garden and eating its bounty as some of the high points, although it is clear that he is the main workhorse when it comes to the daily chores such an endeavor requires. After some recent rainy weather, he describes getting down on his knees to do the necessary weeding. His work has been noticed on Pine Mountain and beyond. Members of the Turner family mentioned him in their interview as someone I should talk to, and then I got a call from Bill Best telling me he had met Walden at a seed swap at Pine Mountain Settlement School. In addition to putting up produce for his family, he sells his abundance to observant neighbors. He says, "These people is begging me, callin' me [for] 'beans, beans.' And if I had this whole thing planted I could sell every bit of it, every bean I had."

Although the garden alone would be enough to keep Walden busy, he takes pride and joy in his other work outdoors. He cuts timber, often seven days a week. He knows it's risky (it's the second most dangerous job, he explains, commercial fishing being the first), but he loves it. He relates the details of close calls with "rattlers" as big as his arm and a near-death experience involving a limb that struck him in the neck and earned him a helicopter ride to the University of Kentucky (UK) hospital (and made him a believer in wearing hard hats). Oh, and his fear of lizards? Perhaps he owes that to an artery sliced by glass while catching "water dogs" as a boy. He couldn't walk by the time his parents got him to the hospital and recalls, "I was just about bled to death."

Walden tends his garden after he gets home from work, but there is one thing that keeps him from working seven days a week: collecting ginseng. "I love ginsengin'. And that's when I don't work very many Saturdays. Saturdays, Sundays I'm out there ginsengin'. That's somethin' I like to do."

Walden and his wife chat about what retirement might look like. He's a homebody, but she wants "to go do things on the weekends. I don't want to sit home." For now, she's just trying to get Walden to go to the Smokies, that helicopter ride to UK being the furthest he's ever been from home. His response: "I just ain't one to go. Just ain't nothing that excites me." They discuss her feelings about moving to the lake house he built from lumber he sawed himself. She admits it's a beautiful place, but it's about three miles off the blacktop road. She concedes, "Maybe when I'm really old I might." I wonder what retirement could possibly be for Walden. Perhaps some porch sitting, but certainly lots of gardening and working in the woods too, as long as he can. He says, "I've got to stay busy. I just cannot sit still. And I know what I'm gonna do the next day when I get up. I know what I'm doin' at work. My brain, it always . . . I done got it thought out."

One of Walden's numerous plots (with garden shed in the background).

Walden holds a box of ginseng he collected and set out to dry.

## DELLA SHEPHERD, LETCHER COUNTY

*I didn't think we were doing anything special, it was just the way it was.*

Della lives seven miles from where she grew up and is proud to say that "what they call the Bible Belt" has always been her home. Her hillside property is perfectly trimmed and tidy, thanks to her own hard work (although she dreams about employing sheep to help with this task). Farming was a way of life for Della as she grew up.

Della Shepherd.

She and her siblings "stepped up and done what we should've done. Didn't know any other way." When I interviewed her, Della spoke with great humility, saying farm life was "just simple things like that."

As a little girl, she followed the corn planter to add in the bean seeds, and her mother determined what days they could plant. Della's mother said they couldn't plant on certain days because the signs were in the Head and the beans would "grow up so tall they won't get any beans out of 'em, whereas in the Feet they will bury in the ground and you'll get a good crop." Her family grew "anything you could go to the grocery store nowadays and buy, really." Bell pepper was rare, but it was "a real treat" when they had it. She recalls finding an apple tree in the mountains and taking a mule and sled there so they could bring back apples for Christmas. And she remembers hanging Tommy Toe tomato plants in the basement at the end of the season to bear ripe tomatoes all the way up until November. Della paints such an idyllic picture that it is easy to forget about all the hard work farming requires. "We didn't know no better," she says. "We didn't know we was poor, we thought we was rich."

Della's husband wasn't raised the same way she was and doesn't believe in planting by the signs. But he tried planting corn on different days at the beginning of May (the first three are barren days) and nothing came up, so perhaps he is starting to come around. Della has a number of other examples of planting at the wrong times and seeds rotting in the ground or hacking an apple tree on an ember day and having it die. She recalls, "I planted a whole field one time, over two acres. And every seed rotted, the corn. My husband actually didn't believe I planted seed, [so] he went out and found the rotten seed. . . . Every seed rotted, it was when the signs was in the Bowels, or [it] might've been an ember day for all I knew, but anyway, they all rotted." In general, she follows her mother's advice to plant when the signs are in the Knees or below.

Della also described a link between the signs and how a plant grows and produces— something else she learned from her mother and something I had heard from others. Della explained that she and her husband had recently

Della's hillside home. She uses chicken-wire enclosures to protect her blueberry bushes from deer.

been on their hands and knees harvesting beans that had been planted in the Feet, as they produced beans very low, at the base of the plant, first. The ones planted in the Head had flowered at the top of the plant first, and they were still waiting for those beans to appear. (Della thinks this finally made a believer out of her husband.) If canning or other preserving is to be done, you definitely want to avoid the Bowels, and for digging potatoes, it is important to do so on a new moon, when the moisture is low, so they don't rot where any cuts are made.

Della is an avid learner, always with an eye toward making things a little easier on herself as she gets older. She has been attending Grow Appalachia meetings at Pine Mountain Settlement School, which she credits for teaching her the importance of keeping farming records. Now she writes everything down on her calendar so she can keep track. She is doing more succession planting, putting in some crops each month when the signs are right, so she'll have plants that are bearing throughout the growing season. "We had so much when I was growing up, that we had to do acres. Now I can just plant a hundred-foot row and do it when the signs come back each month into the Feet. I can time it and play with it now, and I've learned just a little will get you just as much as that acre would if I do it in the right times."

# DEBBIE COOK, LETCHER COUNTY

*I can't ever say there was a year when our garden failed, and we planted by the signs. That's kind of what makes me believe in it because I don't remember us ever having a bad year with anything.*

Debbie Cook moved to her home at the old Apex coal camp in Letcher County thirty years ago from the suburbs of Indianapolis. At the time she arrived, she was being the "obedient wife" because her husband (now her ex) wanted to move back home.

Debbie Cook.

He has since left the area, while she remains. Debbie's home and garden are on a thin strip of bottomland along the North Fork of the Kentucky River, but most of her thirty acres remains wooded. To visitors, her gardening approach appears whimsical but tidy. She grows a huge variety of plants and is always looking for new and interesting additions. When I visited in September, her many different varieties of squash and gourds were sprawling along the ground and up some structures (despite her claims that it hadn't been a good year for squash).

For about a decade Debbie gardened alongside her mother-in-law, Josephine Spangler Cook. Josephine's instructions were clear: Plant in the Breast or Neck, and never plant in the Bowels or Feet. Peas should be planted on Valentine's Day. Harvesting must be done in the morning while it is still damp, and planting is typically done in the evening. Debbie recalls with a smile Josephine's familiarity with the audacity of the crows in the area. When planting corn, she insisted that each kernel be quickly covered, lest the crows start cawing, "Plantin' corn! Plantin' corn!" to alert the masses. Josephine considered the use of a farmer's almanac, which tells readers when to do things, a form of cheating; instead, she used a calendar from the local garden supply store. Debbie still uses a similar one put out by the Letcher County Soil Conservation District. Debbie's Pennsylvania Dutch and

Swiss Mennonite ancestors brought two books with them—an almanac and a Bible. "And that kind of floored me to think that 300 years ago . . . they were studying the stars and planting stuff. I feel like it's kind of part of my heritage because I'm a little bit more than half German. And I know that [to] my ancestors that was important . . . [so] it becomes more important to me."

Debbie has become increasingly interested in medicinal herbs and forest farming and spends time researching those subjects. Her property has hosted Grow Appalachia workshops on forest farming, and she dreams of growing ginseng one day. She tells about curing a stubborn inner ear infection by drinking calendula tea daily. Her concern about what she was putting in and on her body led to an interest in natural

Calendula flowers drying for use in Debbie's next batch of salve or as a healing tea.

skin-care products; she eventually started making her own and giving them as gifts. Encouragement from coworkers who used the products led Debbie to get her cosmetics license and create her own brand called Mountain Girls Skincare. She now sells the products at the farmers' market and by direct sales through word of mouth. Although this endeavor started as a fun hobby, she takes her business quite seriously. Debbie creates her products in a commercial kitchen and treats them as if they were going to be eaten. In addition to general skin-care items such as body cream and face serum, she makes a calendula salve that she can't keep in stock. "I became interested in the calendula flower because it's an antifungal and antiseptic. In the early 1900s if you got a cut and you went to the doctor they would give you a prescription for calendula salve, and you would take that to the pharmacist and they would make you some calendula salve. . . . Well, I can't keep enough of my calendula salve, and I'm a believer in it."

Debbie's growing interest in medicinal herbs means that she is learning to plant by the signs for things other than vegetables. Her research indicates that Libra (Kidneys) and Virgo (Bowels) are good for aromatic herbs and flowers, so she tries to plant herbs at those times. Because her garden is increasingly occupied by medicinal plants, she has expanded her planting area into the forested hillside as well. Like others I interviewed, Debbie seeks a balance between continuing the lessons learned from her mother-in-law and nurturing new interests that allow her to learn more. "It's all so much work. And it's very fulfilling to can ninety quarts of green beans, but it's also kind of cool to make some salve that'll heal your skin. So I'm trying to get a happy balance."

## GLENN BROWN, LETCHER COUNTY

Mom would say plant when the signs was here. Sometimes Dad would, [but] sometimes he'd say, "I'll plant when the signs is in the ground." He always raised a crop, but both of them, even Dad, wouldn't plant when the signs was in the Bowels.

Glenn Brown can tell you about clearing trees on his great-great-grandfather's land grant—a three-mile swath of hillside—to grow corn. He is happy to explain why corn is "the staff of life." "Everything eat corn. . . . My dad would take a hundred-pound bag of corn to the mill [and] have it ground up like cornmeal." This would be used to make cornbread for the family and to feed the milk cow and the hogs. "Back then, when we'd go to school, 'bout everybody at school, the kids, had a four-gallon lard bucket. They'd pour the milk, and everybody'd sit around and eat with their spoon, their milk and [crumbled up corn] bread for school." Hominy was made from corn. Corn was cracked for chickens. The leaves and stalks became fodder for the milk cow and the old mule. Corncobs were made into pipes. They would also fry up "green" corn, given that they "didn't have no sweet corn back in them days." Shucks became mattresses, which Glenn recalls sleeping on when visiting his grandpa in Barbourville.

Wildlife also took advantage of the abundant crop covering the hillsides, as land clearing and farming expanded. "You couldn't get all of the corn, some of it you'd leave, them old nubbins or something. Quail liked all of that in there. I'd say he [his great-great-grandfather] had eight to twelve coveys of quail in his land, and every field you'd go to, some fields had two coveys of quail in them." Glenn describes popping out of the woods into a field and

Glenn Brown.

startling a covey—the dozen or so birds would defend themselves by circling around with their heads sticking out. Rabbits also nested in the cornfields and would be seen frequently. Canned whole-kernel corn would be used to "chum the fish with it, ya know." But, Glenn admits, "I guess the main thing you had that corn for, though, was to make corn whiskey out of it, moonshiners." A little-known function of tall "Indian corn" that Glenn still utilizes is to hide watermelons and cantaloupes from passersby. He can relate to the melon thieves he now aims to deceive. Glenn stole a watermelon from a neighbor when he was a child (his older brother was the ringleader, but he was "aidin' and abettin'"). He worries to this day because the old man who found them after they'd eaten it said he had been saving it for seed.

Four of the thirty-five beans Glenn curates, drying at his home.

Glenn's father worked in the coal mines, so he and his brothers had to tend the gardens if they wanted to eat. "I guess I'm the only one around anywhere that took a likin' to it. But I've liked to ever since then." In addition to corn, his family grew beans and potatoes as the main staples. Added to that was "'bout everything ya grow," including carrots, turnips, rutabagas, tomatoes, squash, and melons. "I used to have forty or fifty things in the garden." They would kill a hog or two each year, and his mother would can sausages and pork chops and smoke big cloth sleeves of sausages that would keep for three or four months in the smokehouse. Glenn enlisted and was a gunner on a tank in World War II, which is why he is hard of hearing. When he returned at around age twenty-five, he got married and started gardening on his own.

Glenn goes by what he has read in most of the almanacs: Breast is best, Loins second, Reins (Kidneys) third, and Feet fourth. In addition to the Bowels, the Head and the Heart are to be avoided. He describes the general approach for aboveground ver-

sus belowground growth: "If you plant potatoes when the moon is raisin' up—ya know, going from nothing up to full—stuff will grow high. [It'll] grow more leaves . . . grow high and everything. But if you plant it on the other side of the moon, potatoes is supposed to be deeper in the ground when you dig." You should also dig potatoes when the moon is going down and the cut places will heal over and store well. A religious man, Glenn links the Bible to good gardening practices—not only planting by the signs but also allowing your garden to rest every seventh year.

Glenn is an avid seed saver and has thirty-five kinds of beans alone. He also saves a potato onion that was his family's. He regrets losing a squash his mother got from her sister in North Carolina around the turn of the twentieth century. He had grown it every year but then lost it about thirty years ago when he planted his last seeds and they didn't come up. And he nearly lost his Hasting cornfield beans the year before my visit, when only three plants came up out of half a row. He got the seeds in late and took great pains to make sure those three plants made it, covering them up when there was danger of frost. He got about a dozen pods out of those three vines, and when I visited, he had a nice row of beans from them. "You talk about being careful. That's one time I was careful about my seeds." He had started growing those beans at around age five or six. For someone who has outlived so many people in his life, Glenn does what he can to make sure his seeds make it through his lifetime and beyond.

# Almanacs & Calendars

Well, we used the almanac. My mom, every time she got ready to plant, she'd go look at that almanac and see where the moon and where the signs was.

CLYDE CHARLES

FOR SOMEONE NOT ACCUSTOMED TO LOOKING AT ONE, consulting an almanac or a calendar meant to guide one's farming and other activities is like trying to read Sanskrit, and in fact, some of the symbols look to be about that old. Comparing various calendars, each of which claims to be the most accurate, reveals enough similarities to make a person believe, but enough differences to let a bit of doubt peek through the cracks.

In addition to the moon's phase or quarter and zodiacal sign, many of these almanacs and calendars include weather predictions, fishing outlooks, sunrise and sunset and moonrise and moonset times, places to record livestock breeding dates and gestation charts, recommendations for first-aid care, when to cut hair, and a number of "special days" most often with religious affiliations. Almanacs may also contain tips of various sorts, recipes, information on new plant varieties, advertisements, short articles on diverse topics, and even poetry and short stories. All calendars and almanacs typically have pages that highlight good days to do certain things, such as when to plant aboveground or belowground crops or when to kill pests.

What differentiates calendars and almanacs is the format—almanacs are in book form and typically have more supplemental information (such as articles or recipes), while calendars are based on almanacs and offer some (but typically not all) of the information almanacs contain.

## ALMANACS

We've all heard of the farmer's almanac, but it turns out there are numerous farmer's almanacs. Subtle differences in their names and the dates they originated distinguish them. Most employ their own astrologers, astronomers, and meteorologists. They typically contain information not only about gardening activities but also about fishing, egg setting, and various other topics. Each almanac has its own slightly different tone, and each has its own special (and of course, most accurate) way of calculating things like weather predictions. What follows is a summary of each of the almanacs encountered during this project. It is certainly not an exhaustive list of all available almanacs, but it provides a sample of the common similarities and differences.

## The Old Farmer's Almanac

And even members of our family have called when they were facing surgeries and they would ask us, "Well, where's the sign going to be? What's the best time of the month, next month, for me to have surgery?" And of course we would go to *The Old Farmer's Almanac*, which is kind of a handbook I guess for individuals that garden by the signs, and we would refer to that and say, "You know on such and such a day in October would be the best time to have that surgery performed."

GARY EASTON

*The Old Farmer's Almanac* (founded in 1792 but first published in 1793) is perhaps the most well known of the farmer's almanacs. Its pale yellow cover features Benjamin Franklin and founder Robert B. Thomas. Thomas began the almanac after spending some years studying and being fascinated by astronomy.[1] He aimed to make his almanac more accurate than the *New England Almanac*, produced by Isaiah Thomas (and his son) between 1775 and 1819. Prior to that, Benjamin Franklin had published *Poor Richard's Almanack* between 1732 and 1758. Franklin's work was the first of its kind and served as the basis for Robert Thomas's publication, which is why Franklin is honored on the cover. *The Old Farmer's Almanac* was well received when it first came out and has remained quite popular, claiming to be "the oldest continuously published periodical in North America," with a print distribution of more than 3 million copies.[2] It is published by Yankee Publishing out of Dublin, New Hampshire. Businesses can advertise in *The Old Farmer's Almanac*, but its distribution model does not feature custom business advertisements on the cover.

*The Old Farmer's Almanac* acknowledges the differences between astrology and astronomy. Although it bases its "Best Days" on the astrological moon sign (using the tropical system), it also provides the moon's astronomical placement in monthly tables. The gardening-related tasks assigned to dates in *The Old Farmer's Almanac* are listed as follows: plant, transplant, and graft; harvest; build/fix fences or garden beds; control insect pests, plow, and weed; and prune. The geographic scope for gardening activities is the continental United States and Canada; this large area is divided into four zones or areas numbered from south to north. The almanac contains a detailed table listing the most common vegetables and crops and summariz-

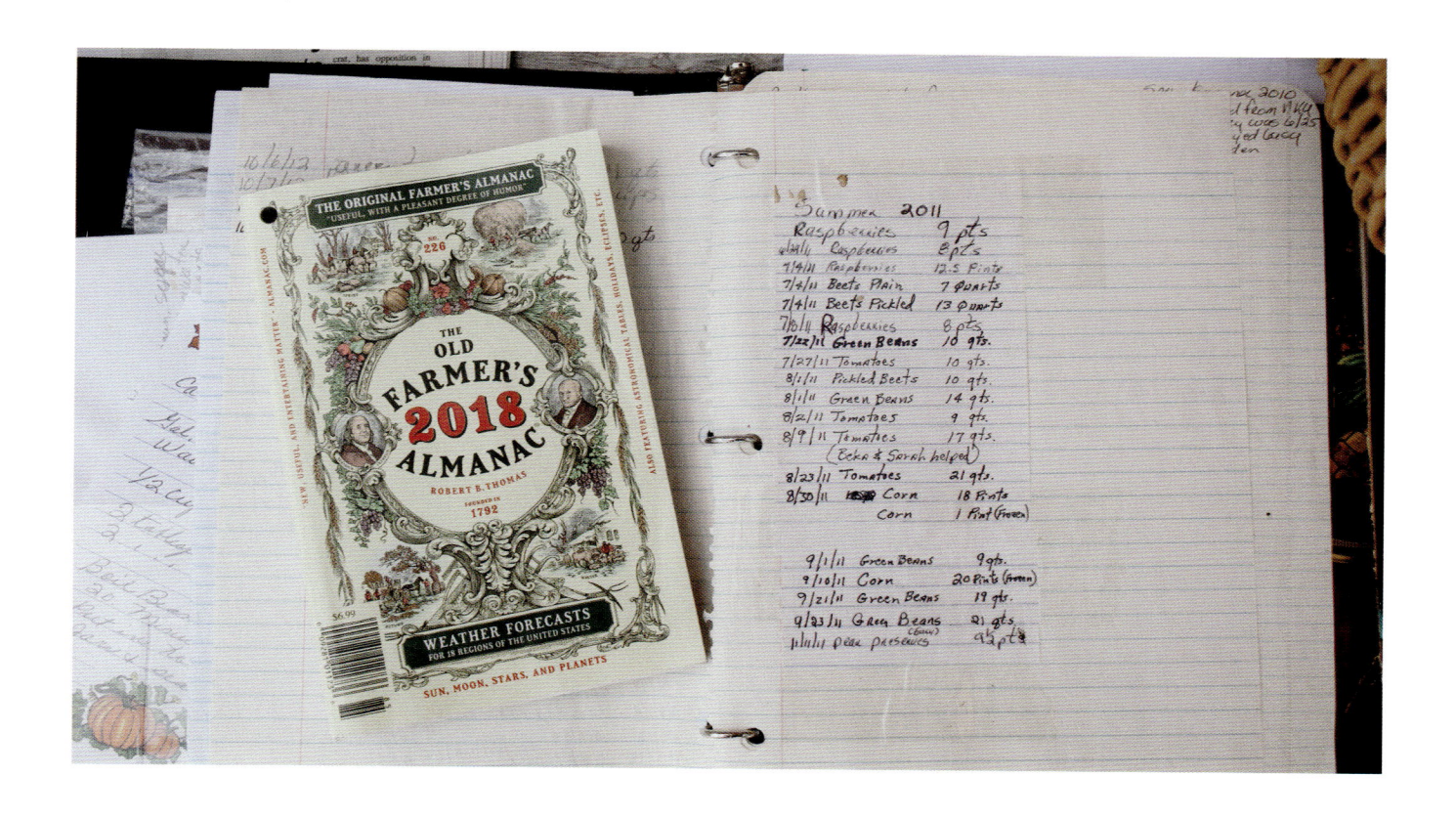

The Eastons' copy of *The Old Farmer's Almanac* alongside their gardening notes.

ing the most favorable dates for planting them in each of the four areas. In addition, a separate "Best Days" table includes numerous activities unrelated to gardening, such as baking, making sauerkraut, coloring hair, starting or ending projects, and buying a home. Detailed weather predictions are given for all fifty states, with eighteen separate zones being designated.

## Farmers' Almanac

This almanac was founded by David Young in 1818 and is published in Lewiston, Maine. It is considerably shorter than *The Old Farmer's Almanac*. The orange cover features a rooster atop a weather vane. Its advice for gardening according to the moon includes the following categories: plant aboveground crops, plant root crops, transplant, plant seedbeds, plant flowers, kill plant pests. Its "Best Days" table has many of the same activities as *The Old Farmer's Almanac*, although *Farmers' Almanac* lists them under the following categories: cooking/baking, health & beauty, parenting, home maintenance, outdoor chores, farm/animal, advertise, and travel & more. The table for planting by the moon signs is astrological, but the moon's astronomical placement is provided in the monthly pages, as well as the five additional constellations included in *The Old Farmer's Almanac*.[3] It also has a fishing calendar and some recipes and general interest articles, although much fewer than in *The Old Farmer's Almanac*. Weather predictions in *Farmers' Almanac* cover the contiguous United States, separated into six zones. *Farmers' Almanac* often serves as an outreach tool for businesses, which can buy them in bulk at a reduced cost and have their business information printed on the cover. Many businesses use this as a marketing tool and a giveaway for customers (similar to calendars, as discussed later).

## Baer's Agricultural Almanac & Gardener's Guide

This almanac is published by John Baer's Sons in Lancaster, Pennsylvania, with astronomical information provided by Hart Wright Company in Lewiston, Maine.[4] The color of the cover changes year by year, but it always features an oval image with two women, wheat, and a single moldboard plow, as well as a rose in the top left corner. Although no one interviewed for this project uses this almanac, it is apparently the main one consulted by Amish farmers.[5] Kentucky is home to many Amish communities scattered throughout the nonmountainous parts of the state, populated by some well-respected and productive farmers. This almanac is unique in that it contains only a handful of advertisements on the inside cover (but none in the body). Except for the outside cover, the entire publication is simple black print on white paper. It can be obtained by mailing a check to the publisher or purchasing it at one of the establishments that carries it (presumably available most commonly in Amish country). Its one page on planting covers the following categories: crops bearing yield above the ground, crops bearing yield below the ground, flower gardens, start seedbeds, and best dates for killing briars, poison ivy, weeds, and pests. *Baer's Agricultural Almanac* also contains short articles on new varieties of vegetables and, like all the others, long-range weather forecasts. These forecasts cover the contiguous United States, summarizing activities for broad regions such as the Southern States,

Northeast, East Coast, Carolinas, Great Plains, Rockies, and so forth. Monthly tables include the moon's place as one of the twelve zodiacal constellations.

## Llewellyn's Moon Sign Book

*My moon sign book is . . . really a unique book. It helps you figure out, you know, if you want to cut your hair at a certain time to increase growth or decrease growth. . . . We use it for advertising and even, you know, . . . when to cut the timber, like I've done that before. . . . I mean, it's just an incredible amount of information. . . . They'll have you look at the aspects where the planets are and what moon sign it's in. And also if it's a good day for you, there is either a big U, a big F or a little u or a little f [standing for unfavorable or favorable] and sometimes nothing. So you know . . . for traveling you would want to pick a good sign for you where it was a big F, so you would have a favorable day.*

JANE POST

The first author of this almanac, produced annually since 1905, was a man named Llewellyn George, who became a well-regarded figure in the world of astrology. Published by Llewellyn Publications out of Woodbury, Minnesota, it is more extensive than the previously discussed almanacs, chock-full of astrological wisdom and astronomical information. Its contents are based on the tropical zodiac system, and it features extensive information about doing almost everything. The subtitle, *Plan Your Life by the Cycles of the Moon*, explains precisely the type of guidance it provides. It features a weekly almanac section with the exact times for each moon sign and the activities that match each one, as well as space to make notes. It also contains many articles and explanations of astrological phenomena, such as when the moon is "void of course" during transitions between each of the twelve signs, and it warns, "Plans or decisions made now often do not pan out." The book also features information on when planets are in retrograde, with Mercury being the one that "rules thought and communication, so it is advisable not to sign important papers, initiate important business or legal work, or make crucial decisions during these times."[6] Its "Good Timing" monthly tables are quite extensive, and it offers even more guidance in the section on choosing the best times for certain activities (which are much more wide ranging than in the almanacs previously discussed). Weather forecasts in *Llewellyn's Moon Sign Book* cover the United States, which is broken into eight zones. Predictions are given for each quarter of the moon's cycle (or each week) in the year.

## The Maria Thun Biodynamic Almanac and Stella Natura Calendar

Biodynamics originated in Germany, and it's very precisely laid out for you. And so, in a way, that doesn't aid you in learning or understanding how these connections were made when you go by the calendar, because you just look at the calendar—Oh, it's a flower sign, can't plant. You know, it's all determined for you. . . . The detail on a calendar that they get into, it's pretty intense. . . . One of the benefits . . . is that the calendar is just packed full of information. It's gotten me to understand the fluid nature of the zodiac and the stars in the sky and appreciate new constellations and understand and see them.

SUSANA LEIN

Rudolf Steiner (1861–1925) was a famous Austrian scientist, philosopher, and thinker who developed a belief system termed anthroposophy or spiritual science, which viewed the earth as a living being under the influence of many great cosmic forces.[7] After being asked to teach a course about his approach focusing on agriculture, Steiner gave a series of eight famous lectures in 1924. These lectures are summarized in the book *Agriculture*, which was published in English in 1993. Steiner's lectures would become the basis for biodynamics, which provided a counter to the prevailing mechanistic and empirical approach to agriculture. Reading Steiner's work can be quite challenging, but it is clear that his belief system emphasizes interactions between the sun, earth, moon, and other planets, with the moon's influence being mediated through water.

Maria Thun (1922–2012) spent decades, starting in the 1940s, testing Steiner's theories. With her husband Walter (and other biodynamic farmers in her region), she directed and took part in trials to test everything related to agriculture: planting dates, harvesting dates, dates for the creation and application of compost and biodynamic preparations, and so forth. She studied astronomy as she conducted this work, which allowed her to look for correlations with cosmic phenomena. Thun's studies resulted in a system of planting based on the zodiac, with each of the twelve constellations having one of the following affinities: root, leaf, flower, or fruit. Her system was based on the constellational zodiac, so the length of the time period associated with each sign varies and overlaps very little with astrological calendars.[8] She also discovered that the moon's perigee and nodes have negative effects. This work became the basis of the biodynamic calendar.

There are two main printed sources for this calendar. They both follow the same general principles just laid out (in terms of which signs favor leaf, fruit, root, and flower) but vary in their calculations and in the specifics related to unfavorable times. *The Maria Thun Biodynamic Almanac* is available in twenty-seven languages, attesting to its widespread use.[9] The *Stella Natura* biodynamic calendar is also based on Thun's work, and this is the calendar routinely used by Susana Lein.[10] Each has monthly pages listing the times (to the hour) for each constellation, as well as solar, lunar, and planetary aspects. There are no universally bad or barren signs in this system; instead, those periods are dictated by eclipses, nodes, perigee, and the like and are shown as unfavorable times scattered throughout each month. Both the almanac and the calendar present daily information in graphic form for easy interpretation. Both sources also include diagrams that depict the constellations of the zodiac as well as those just outside of it. *The Maria Thun Biodynamic Almanac* contains monthly diagrams that show the moon's celestial placement each day of the year, as if the moon is riding a wave on the horizon. The *Stella Natura* calendar contains one diagram for the year, with placement of the sun indicated for the solstices and equinoxes.

## CALENDARS

While many of the almanac publishers are located in the northeastern or central United States, most calendar publishers are in the South, with many having roots in Tennessee. Three companies publish the calendars pulled out during the interviews conducted for this project.[11] All claim to be the publisher of the "original" almanac calendar, started in 1876. One source is Ramon's Brownie Calendars in Le Roy, New York, although the first Brownie calendar was printed by the Brown Manufac-

Susana Lein consults one of the monthly pages in the *Stella Natura* calendar.

turing Company in Greeneville, Tennessee. That calendar was an advertisement for the company's medicines and featured a little doctor carrying a bag of Ramon's pills. The company was later bought by David Grayson in Le Roy, and although it no longer sold patent medicines, the calendar had become such a staple throughout the South and Midwest that he continued to print it. It apparently continued in Tennessee as well, with the American Calendar Company, which shares its roots with Ramon's, still printing calendars today in Clarksville. In addition, a calendar put out by Francis & Lusky Company of Nashville, Tennessee, is mentioned in *The Foxfire Book*, and the company still prints promotional calendars today. A fourth offering is *The Weather Vane [Almanac] Calendar*, published by Drum-Line (formerly Drummond Printing Inc.) out of Stuttgart, Arkansas.

The companies sell their calendars wholesale to businesses, customizing the top sections of the monthly pages to advertise each buyer's business. These calendars became an early marketing or promotional tool for numerous businesses throughout the United States. Because they are designed to promote the local business that distributes them, rather than the calendar company itself, it is sometimes difficult or even impossible to locate the publisher on the calendar.

In these calendars, each day typically contains the moon's sign (the twelve standard zodiac constellations), sunrise and sunset times, moonrise (and sometimes moonset) times, weather predictions, fishing outlook, and length of day. Some include daily gardening information; others include that information in a monthly section. It is typically unclear which zodiacal system or what almanac a calendar is based on.

## CALENDAR CULTURE

Growing up, all the little country stores—and I'm gonna say, most of them were maybe ten miles apart—they were frequent, they would have in the fall what everybody referred to as a Brownie calendar. Their loyal customers, as they came and went, that was their little gift to them. And the Brownie calendar was real detailed in the different folklore or legend or whatever. It had your signs, good nights for fishing, the moon cycles and phases, it's got all that information—it is an almanac. A lot of people use those, certain signs you don't plant in, certain signs you do plant in, and they used those calendars.

ANITA TOLLIVER

Perhaps as important as the information in the calendar itself is the ritual of getting a new one every fall. Everyone has a favorite source they rely on each year. In the past, such calendars were available at all the local general stores or even banks, but today, the most common sources seem to be hardware stores and funeral homes. These calendars have space at the top for these businesses to advertise. In conducting interviews for this project, it quickly became clear that the calendar is often an important guide for gardening activities as well as a place to keep records. More than one person revealed a stack of old calendars they were hanging on to because of the gardening records they contained. Some spoke of the excitement of getting the next year's calendar around Halloween or early November. They are a hot commodity, and by the time spring comes around, they can be quite difficult to find. One per-

son I interviewed gave me a copy of the calendar he uses and explained that he had to call in some favors to get it, and the folks working at the farm supply store had to go in the back and find it—after all, our interview took place in early May.

## TESTING THE CLAIMS

For the most part, all almanacs and calendars claim to be the best and cite their large distribution as testament to their accuracy. T. E. Black says in his "Lifetime Planting, Business, and Fishing Guide": "I made a 13-year test for the right signs for planting all crops, business and fishing and other things and for the correct dates I found The Ladies Birthday Almanac and others that correspond with it are most correct."[12]

*The Old Farmer's Almanac* starts its weather section with a summary entitled "How Accurate Was Our Forecast Last Winter?" which compares the previous year's predictions with the actual weather. It shows data for one city in each of the eighteen regions (the cities change from year to year) and reports its accuracy in predicting precipitation and temperature in the previous winter. The almanac claims a long-term accuracy rate of 80 percent.

**FACING:** Beehives next to a pasture.

In *Planetary Planting* Louise Riotte gives numerous accounts of personal successes and failures to convince readers to follow her system, which closely aligns with that of *Llewellyn's Moon Sign Book*.[13] She opens her book with a tale of wading out "when the garden was a sea of mud" to plant corn, despite her husband's ridicule, for "it was the *right* sign and the right *phase* and I was bound and determined to plant." And (of course) she ended up with a wonderful sweet corn harvest, while all her neighbors experienced failures. Riotte discusses her experience planting by the signs and doing so organically for more than thirty years; she includes recommendations for when to start and turn compost heaps. She writes, "Organic gardening practices teach us *how* to plant in harmony with nature; astrology teaches us *when*. The knowledge of how to plant combined with when to plant will give us much better results than when one is used without the other."[14]

For those readers who are interested in seeing test results, the many published works of Maria Thun are worth a look. In *Results from the Biodynamic Sowing and Planting Calendar,* Thun describes decades of planting trials conducted to arrive at her calendar system. Although the initial trials were done with radishes, she used a wide array of plants over her long tenure, and the variety of work is quite extensive. *The Biodynamic Year* is a more recently published book that covers even more decades of Thun's experience. The depth of her work and its record is unrivaled. As an example, the variables tested in her studies on making compost include starting with different animal manure types, collecting the manure on different days, and applying the finished product on different days. Her work also covers oil crops and their yield and when to prepare and apply different biodynamic preparations. She also studied beekeeping and winemaking quite extensively. Her family carries on this work and continues to publish her writing (see the bibliography).

The next chapter covers all the signs and what gardening activities should be conducted under each one, but a few examples come up rather frequently and could provide some interesting results if you'd like to conduct your own tests. Cucumbers planted in flowering signs are said to be all flowers and no fruit. If corn is planted in the light of the moon (especially during the first quarter), the ears will stay upright and rot, whereas if it is planted later in the cycle, the ears will drop down so they shed water better and won't rot. And finally, potatoes—in terms of both planting and harvesting—are said to produce quite different results depending on which side of the full moon these activities are performed.

# The Signs

IN COMPILING RECOMMENDATIONS FROM THE DIFFERENT CALENDARS USED, as well as recommendations from the interviewees themselves, it quickly becomes apparent that there is disagreement regarding which signs are good (and bad) for various gardening activities. Perhaps that shouldn't be surprising, given the different systems used and the dependence on oral and practiced traditions. However, some patterns do emerge. This chapter presents information gleaned from the interviews, calendars, almanacs, and other sources about the signs and special days. Despite the differing interpretations, depending on which source you consult or who you speak with, certain themes emerged during my research (and I do not endorse any one version over another).

## MOON PHASES

But most [of] the time you can 'bout look at the moon and tell. You can look at that moon, if that moon's full you know, you think, you start watching that moon [as] it comes up. You can tell a half moon, you know, and you see the moon and the quarter.

WALDEN WHITEHEAD

To those who regularly plant by the signs, the presence of the moon in the night (and sometimes day) sky is a reminder of the passage of time and of gardening tasks to plan. Almanacs and calendars provide a roadmap of what's to come, but glancing up is never a bad idea either, and it can help you stay on course.

## Light versus Dark

Now if you dig potatoes, if you cut 'em when the moon is full going down like that, you'd cut 'em and most—half of 'em or two-thirds—of the ones you cut would be healed back up. Stay all winter with a cut place some of 'em. So, I believe in that some too.

**GLENN BROWN**

The most basic aspect of planting by the signs involves the two halves of the moon's cycle. It is widely held that these halves influence aboveground and belowground crops. That is, plants whose harvestable portion is above the ground should be planted in the growing or waxing part of the cycle (between new and full), whereas those whose harvestable portion is below the ground should be planted in the decreasing or waning part of the cycle (between full and new). Interviewees also referred to these two halves as the moon going up or going down or being light or dark. The general thinking is that the downward pull desirable for good root growth is stronger during the dark half, while planting during the light half results in more vigorous aboveground growth. Most almanacs and calendars account for this difference by designating separate times for the planting of aboveground and belowground crops.

Harvesting was another common topic among the interviewees, with potatoes being mentioned frequently. In general, most agreed that potatoes should be both planted and harvested when the moon is decreasing, or going down.[1] *The Old Farmer's Almanac* specifies that pruning during the waxing moon results in increased growth, while pruning during the waning moon decreases growth. The biodynamic calendar suggests that fruit be harvested during a fruit sign in the ascending moon, but this is different from the waxing and waning parts of the moon's cycle—it has to do with the moon's position on the horizon during the cycle. As previously discussed, the biodynamic calendar is markedly different from the others because it is based on the constellational zodiac (see previous chapter).

Potatoes at the farmers' market.

## Quarters

*But your corn, and your taters and stuff, I go in the old part of the moon.
You know, or up in like a third quarter or something like that. A lot of
people don't believe that. But now it's true.*

**WALDEN WHITEHEAD**

The moon's quarters are thought to embody certain qualities or elements. For example, during the full moon, water is considered to be most available and seeds are best able to absorb it. Harvesting of root crops is recommended in the decreasing moon (third or fourth quarter). The last quarter is generally regarded as the most barren, so if you engage in activities to eliminate certain things—such as insect pests or weeds—you will be most successful. Planting is not recommended during the last quarter. Many sources suggest avoiding new or full moon days (a smaller number of sources also include transitional days between quarters), but this is not universal.[2] Many sources cite the second quarter as better for harvesting if you intend to keep the seeds. Some sources base planting times on the seeds' location in the plant. For example, the first quarter is best for those (generally leafy plants) that have seeds "outside the fruit," such as lettuce, spinach, broccoli, and grains.[3] The second quarter is best for plants that produce seed within the fruit, such as tomatoes, beans, squash, and peppers. Nobe Baker suggests planting beans and corn in the new of the moon, as they will grow tall; in contrast, potatoes should be planted at the full moon to encourage short vines, with most of the growth being directed to the tubers.

## THE ZODIAC

Layering the zodiac signs over the moon phases makes things interesting. Those people with the most experience planting by the signs include both the moon's quarter and the zodiac sign in their recommendations.[4] Many others depend on calendars or almanacs that provide specific guidance. Each of the zodiac signs is assigned not only a body part and symbol (see table 1.1) but also an earth element, a climatological quality, and a planet that "rules" the sign (table 4.1), as well as a designation

Table 4.1. Signs of the Zodiac and Related Identifiers

| SIGN | BODY PART | ELEMENT | QUALITY | PLANET |
|---|---|---|---|---|
| Aries | Head | Fire/Warmth | Barren and dry | Mars |
| Taurus | Neck (Throat) | Earth | Productive and moist | Venus |
| Gemini | Arms (Chest) | Air/Light | Barren and dry | Mercury |
| Cancer | Breast (Stomach) | Water | Very fruitful and moist | Moon |
| Leo | Heart (Back) | Fire/Warmth | Very barren and dry | Sun |
| Virgo | Bowels | Earth | Barren and moist | Mercury |
| Libra | Kidneys/Reins | Air/Light | Semifruitful and moist | Venus |
| Scorpio | Loins/Secrets | Water | Very fruitful and moist | Mars |
| Sagittarius | Thighs | Fire/Warmth | Barren and dry | Jupiter |
| Capricorn | Knees | Earth | Productive and dry | Saturn |
| Aquarius | Legs (Ankles) | Air/Light | Barren and dry | Uranus |
| Pisces | Feet | Water | Productive and moist | Neptune |

*Note:* The body part names are fairly consistent in multiple sources; those in parentheses are less common. The elements and qualities are from Catterall's *Gardening by the Moon* calendar (but match those listed in many other sources). The planet associations are from Wigginton, *Foxfire Book*.

of either feminine or masculine. Weather predictions in almanacs rely in part on these designations, as well as interactions of the planets.

Four signs are mentioned most consistently as being good or fruitful signs: Taurus/Neck, Cancer/Breast (most fruitful), Scorpio/Loins/Secrets, and Pisces/Feet. Phil Case uses a mnemonic device—Signs Plant Thick Crops—to help him remember the four good signs (Scorpio, Pisces, Taurus, and Cancer). During the interviews, many people discussed the Feet (Pisces) and Breast (Cancer) as good signs to plant in; Taurus and Scorpio came up much less frequently. Some sources suggest that transplanting should be done in a water or earth sign (not an air or fire sign).

As with the good signs, there is a lack of agreement on what the barren signs are—that is, those times when it is inadvisable to plant and you should focus your energies on destroying pests or simply resting. However, certain patterns emerge, and the most frequently mentioned barren signs are Aries/Head, Leo/Heart, and Virgo/Bowels.

The biodynamic calendar is quite different from the others. Because it uses the constellational zodiac, there is a considerable disconnect with astrological calendars in terms of when the moon is in which sign. In addition, the biodynamic calendar assigns one of the four plant parts (fruit, root, flower, leaf) to each sign, indicating the favorable times for that part. Thus, no signs are considered bad; rather, unfavorable times or blackout days are governed by other factors and can occur in any sign.

The following sections offer recommendations for each of the signs based on consulting thirteen published works (calendars, almanacs, and books) and the twenty-two people interviewed. Only tasks related to gardening are included.

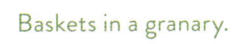

## Aries/Head

*They was three phases that all the almanacs and . . . calendars didn't want you to plant: when the signs was in the Bowels or in the Head or in the Heart.*

GLENN BROWN

Nearly all references say that Aries is not a good sign to plant in; instead, it is a good time to destroy weeds and pests. Some sources emphasize these activities only in the third or fourth quarter, while planting crops with vines or stalks is favored during the first and second quarters. Harvesting of fruit and root crops is allowable, according to some sources (ideally, in the third or fourth quarter if they are to be stored). Two sources say that pruning is appropriate in this sign, but one specifies it should be done in the third quarter. Planting is recommended for onions in two print sources, while the planting of cabbage, beets, and tobacco is listed in one source each. Four people interviewed mentioned this sign, and all said they wouldn't plant anything in it.

The biodynamic calendar differs in some ways when it comes to Aries, which is designated a fruit sign. It agrees that harvesting fruits (anything that bears seeds) should be done in the third or fourth quarter under Aries or any other fruit sign. But it also allows the planting of crops whose fruit is to be harvested under this sign (quite a long list, including many common garden plants).

## Taurus/Neck

*We would watch the calendar and the only time that we ever planted anything was in the sign of the Breast or the Neck . . . you didn't garden unless it was in that right sign to plant.*

DEBBIE COOK

Many written sources consider Taurus one of the four most fruitful (or good) signs, although it was mentioned by only two people interviewed (Phil Case and Debbie Cook). Louise Riotte writes that this sign is fairly productive and confers

special hardiness to crops planted under it, meaning that they can better tolerate extreme conditions.[5] She lists potatoes and other root crops, as well as cabbage, lettuce, and other leafy vegetables, as being favored in Taurus, as do a number of other print sources. Flowers are also mentioned in a handful of sources as being favored under this sign. Taurus is one of the four signs during which grafting is recommended in *The Old Farmer's Almanac*. The biodynamic calendar designates Taurus a root sign.

Winter squash and melons.

## Gemini/Arms

*When we were growing up, Mom would plant the beans when the signs was in the Arms, Twin days. But I always try to plant mine [in] Cancer/Breast; [it's] the best time that I know of to plant 'em. . . . Actually, the Secrets are better than the Cancer/Breast.*

**MARY OVERBEY**

In many ways, the sign Gemini captures the complexity of planting by the signs. Nine of the thirteen written sources refer to Gemini as a barren, dry sign in which seeds tend to rot. Two sources make an exception for melons. And one calendar (with no publisher listed) provides conflicting information; it states that "any seed planted now will tend to rot" on each day during Gemini, but the front matter claims Gemini favors beans and cucumbers. T. E. Black says of this sign, "I find it one of the second-best signs for planting and transplanting all crops, root crops, and crops that bear above the ground."[6] The biodynamic calendar designates Gemini a flower sign, so only flowers should be planted under it.

If there is one crop associated with Gemini/Arms, it is beans. Beans have been an incredibly important food source for people in Appalachia throughout its history. Numerous texts and articles discuss heirloom varieties and the nutritional differences between the beans of our ancestors and the bright green hulls everyone has access to in grocery stores.[7] Given its importance, this one crop can serve as a case study for the practice of planting by the signs. Seven of the people interviewed mentioned planting beans in the Arms/Gemini. Some wholeheartedly endorsed it, including Phil Case, who said:

The best sign for planting beans is Gemini . . . because they grow as long as your arms, when the moon's in the light phase. Well, the trouble is, we don't have that particular configuration of light in the summer. You'll have a lot of Gemini days and a lot of light moon days, but for them to get together. . . . One of the best bean crops my wife and I had in that first garden was planted in that correct configuration. And I have never in my life seen the number of beans . . . we canned and canned and canned and canned and froze. And finally, [we] just pulled the bean plants up. There is only so many beans that a person can have.

Bill Best has grown more beans than just about anybody, and he learned from his neighbor Lucy Alexander to plant beans in Gemini, noting that they keep a green color when dried. Others expressed some skepticism. Two people mentioned that the "old-timers" used to plant beans in the Arms, but they didn't agree with it or understand why, given their experiences or what they had read. People interviewed for both Foxfire books said beans should be planted in the Arms.[8] So how can this dispute be resolved or explained? Perhaps some calendars have the moon in Gemini when it is actually in Taurus or Cancer—the good signs that come before and after it. Perhaps those people who have had luck planting beans in Gemini have caught the years when that sign coincides with the light part of the moon's phase, which apparently doesn't happen very often. Certainly, some people believe strongly in planting beans in Gemini, and they have stories attesting to their success.

## Cancer/Breast

When I plant my beans when the sign is right, I plant 'em in the Breast 'cause that's the best, in the local calendar or anything I ever seen.

GLENN BROWN

If any one sign is universally considered the best, it is Cancer. All calendars deem it a good sign to plant in, and everyone interviewed said so as well. Cancer is considered a watery and fruitful or bearing sign. One source also mentions that crops planted under this sign are better able to withstand drought. Some sources recommend grafting and irrigating under this sign (in addition to planting and transplanting). *Baer's Agricultural Almanac* suggests planting beans at the full moon under Cancer,

FACING: Beans in a garden.

and Louise Riotte says to plant beans under this sign in the second quarter. The biodynamic calendar designates Cancer a leaf sign.

## Leo/Heart

I could give you one of the negative [examples of] . . . pruning a . . . fruit tree when the sign is in the Heart. . . . I pruned it in the fall and it didn't make it through the next spring. So, I know some people would say, "Well, it probably got diseased and died." Well, it could have. But I know that I was pruning at the wrong time, so that was enough lesson for me.

GARY EASTON

All the print sources I consulted consider Leo a bad sign during which only killing activities should be performed, such as killing pests, cultivating, and the like. None of these sources (other than the biodynamic calendar) suggest any kind of planting, and in fact, they strongly warn against it. The subject came up in five interviews, leading to similar cautions. Leo is considered an excellent sign for destroying pests and, according to a couple of sources, for harvesting.[9] Weeds targeted during the old of the moon in Leo will be more permanently destroyed than at any other time, according to *Baer's Agricultural Almanac*. Finally, one source says that fruit trees can be pruned, but only in the third quarter.[10] Leo is designated a fruit sign in the biodynamic calendar, and unlike other fruit signs, seed formation is positively influenced.

Purple coneflowers.

## Virgo/Bowels

*We never planted anything when it was in the sign of the Bowels. [My mother-in-law] said never, no matter what. You [know] I don't even think we worked in the garden then, when it was in the sign of the Bowels.*

**DEBBIE COOK**

**FACING:** Okra grown for seed.

Five people interviewed brought up Virgo, and all warned against planting any vegetables under this sign. Four published sources and two people interviewed referred to Virgo as being favorable for planting flowers.[11] But as with Leo, gardening activities should generally be confined to controlling plant and animal pests. One calendar says of Virgo, "Never plant or your seeds will rot." Medicinal plants are mentioned in one source as being favored in Virgo.[12] More so than any other sign, Virgo came up in the interviews with regard to preserving or canning, with clear warnings to avoid doing so. The biodynamic calendar designates Virgo a root sign.

## Libra/Kidneys/Reins

Now, if you're looking at the date. So here today . . . these are flowering signs Virgo and Libra, so there are four [days] there, and because of the length of the month, there's some at the end of the month too. So today if you were planting . . . I would suggest . . . putting out tulip bulbs, things like that, things that you want to flower. Now the traditionalists and everything that I've read, Mr. Van Meter too, [say] you don't want to plant vegetables in a flowering sign, because that's what they do [i.e., they flower].

PHIL CASE

Flowers came up most frequently as being favored in Libra, and the biodynamic calendar aligns with this. Quite a few sources also mention herbs. Dividing or planting flowers (or herbs) in Libra was recommended by four interviewees and eight published sources. Some printed sources are even broader, listing both aboveground and belowground crops that are favored. Vines are specifically mentioned in a handful of them. Glenn Brown says Libra is the third best sign in general for planting (after Cancer/Breast and Scorpio/Loins).

## Scorpio/Loins/Secrets

If all things else are equal, in other words, your ground was dry, how hard is it to just say OK, today is a Scorpio day in the light of the moon. And I've got six tomato plants to set out. How hard is it to do that? It's not hard.

PHIL CASE

Most published sources say Scorpio is only slightly less productive than Cancer—that is, it is a very good sign (some consider it equal to Cancer). Vines are mentioned in a couple of sources, and the specific crops cited are corn, tomatoes, squash, onions from seed, and beans in the second quarter. But according to many sources, any aboveground or root crop is favored (matching the phases: growing moon for aboveground, decreasing moon for belowground). Among published sources, only T. E. Black mentioned flow-

ers. A small number of sources note that other gardening activities, such as grafting and irrigation, are likely to be successful under this sign. The biodynamic calendar designates Scorpio a leaf sign, thus favoring all leafy greens and herbs.

## Sagittarius/Thighs

You don't want to plant anything in fourth quarter Sagittarius because you'll kill it.

JULIE MARUSKIN

Most printed sources consider Sagittarius a barren sign, best limited to destroying pests and harvesting, although onions are apparently favored. Louise Riotte also lists garlic, potatoes, peppers, and radishes. T. E. Black mentions onions and cucumbers but warns not to transplant anything. *Baer's Agricultural Almanac* broadly suggests planting root crops, so long as the moon is dark or waning. The biodynamic calendar considers Sagittarius a sign that favors fruit formation.

## Capricorn/Knees

I just [plant] mostly by the signs—any time from the Knees down I try to plant.

DELLA SHEPHERD

Capricorn is good for planting or harvesting root crops, according to most printed sources. Three people interviewed said that planting in the Knees or lower (Legs, Feet) is a good general rule. Louise Riotte lists a wide variety of aboveground and belowground crops, as well as fruit trees and flowers, as being favored. *The Old Farmer's Almanac* suggests that no planting should be done, but it's a good time to fix fences and garden beds. T. E. Black says Capricorn is the number-one sign for all root crops, but it is also good for flowers and aboveground plants. According to the biodynamic calendar, when the moon is in this constellation, root growth is favored.

## Aquarius/Legs

Most of the time they planted when the sign's below the waist and then down in the Leg or the Feet. The Knees is all right.

CLYDE CHARLES

Three people interviewed considered Aquarius a good sign to plant in, whereas all the almanacs and calendars consider it a barren sign. One calendar (no publisher listed) indicated that Aquarius always falls when the moon is neither high nor low. Only one calendar listed any plant as favored: onion.[13] T. E. Black says Aquarius is "very good for planting crops that produce above the ground. Except seeds are apt to rot." The biodynamic calendar designates Aquarius a flower sign, and one almanac lists flowers as being favored under this sign.[14]

## Pisces/Feet

The most fruitful signs are water, which are like Cancer, Pisces . . . Scorpio. So, there's three water signs. And when the moon is in those zodiacal phases, it . . . more than likely will rain, even if it's droughty. So, you know, you want to catch that rain when you're planting your little seedlings.

JANE POST

By all accounts, Pisces is a favorable sign. It is thought to be especially good for planting belowground or root crops, although aboveground plantings are possible as well (especially during the moon's light phase). According to *Baer's Agricultural Almanac*, plants that go in the ground in Pisces are able to withstand drought. There is some controversy over whether potatoes should be planted in this sign. Some sources warn that potatoes planted in Pisces will have toes or nubs, but most recommend planting potatoes in this sign. Louise Riotte has a very long list of favorable crops, including beans when planted in the second quarter. The biodynamic calendar considers Pisces a leaf sign.

Bowl of garlic.

## OTHER FORMULAS

In addition to the specific aspects of each of the zodiac signs, the interviewees mentioned two general formulas for determining when to plant or do other gardening-related activities. Though not very common, they came up more than once and thus are worth considering.

## Knees Down

*But they claimed if you planted . . . in the Heart or Head, it would just grow a little bit right in the top. It wouldn't grow from top to bottom. I mean it wouldn't bear. So, they always said plant it in the Feet and the Knees, no higher than the waist.*

CLYDE CHARLES

The general rule of planting in the signs located in the lower part of the body was mentioned by Clyde Charles, Della Shepherd, and Sarah Epperson. This same general rule is found in many calendars and almanacs, but usually for other purposes such as weaning (discussed in the next chapter). One calendar does say that the seeds of root crops should be planted "during the dark of the moon and in the sign of the lower part of the body."[15] However, most do not mention this formula at all, and some list signs above the waist—namely, the Neck and the Breast—as good times to plant. On the whole, among the five signs from Scorpio down, only one is (largely) considered a barren or killing one: Sagittarius/Thighs. Thus, there are quite a few good or so-so signs in that below-the-waist sequence, so the attraction of using this simple formula is understandable. Myrtle Turner also mentioned this sequence, but in reference to making sauerkraut.

## Anything with Two

*So, [my mother] always said like if you got the two Arms, and the two Breasts, two Legs—anything that has two is where it's good to plant.*

ABBY WALKER

This formula was mentioned in only one interview, when Abby referred to Myrtle Turner's advice. It basically adds the Arms (Gemini) and Breast (Cancer) to the waist-down formula. As previously discussed, some consider the Arms a good sign, and the Breast is universally considered a good sign. However, this general formula would also include the Legs (Aquarius) and Thighs (Sagittarius), which, according to most sources, are not good.[16] It also leaves out the Neck (Taurus), which most published sources consider a good sign but did not come up much in the interviews.

## DOES IT REALLY MATTER?

My brother-in-law . . . was in the hospital and he needed his potatoes planted. Well, you can't do that, it's a bad time, bad time. I looked, and the signs was in the Head. . . . He said, "Plant 'em anyway." We growed potatoes just about as big as a head. . . . It might be in my head, but I still base my plantin' on [the signs]. That year he was blessed to have good potatoes.

DELLA SHEPHERD

Even among those who do their best to plant by the signs, some aren't entirely sure it matters. Four people expressed a bit of skepticism or doubt. Of course, given all the interactions going on in the cosmos and the different ways to interpret or calculate them, it's possible something could be missed. Or perhaps the time is close enough to a favorable sign that the seeds wait until that sign comes and then start to grow rapidly. As Susana Lein explains, "I believe that if a plant or a transplant or whatever goes in the ground on the wrong sign, it might hang out and wait for the explosion that can happen when it gets supported by the right sign. So, yeah, that's the resilience of nature."

## SPECIAL DAYS

Aside from the moon's phases and zodiac signs, a number of specific dates or holidays came up in both the interviews and the calendars and almanacs examined.

### Good Friday

But just recently, I planted some beans on Good Friday. Good Friday is historically the day . . . most people plant their potatoes. But I have . . . several friends who swear by planting beans on Good Friday as well.

BILL BEST

The seasons and differences in day length are due to the tilt of the earth's axis, causing different parts of the globe to be more or less exposed at different times of the year as the earth revolves around the sun. The vernal equinox is the point at which the sun is directly in line with the equator, meaning that the Northern and Southern Hemispheres receive the same amount of light.[17] Although this sounds straightforward, it is actually quite complex, for many of the same reasons that complicate the calculations of moon phases and zodiac signs.[18] For example, Easter is the Sunday that follows the full moon on or after the vernal equinox.[19] This means the date of Easter can vary by more than a month.[20] However, Easter always occurs (regardless of the controversy over when the vernal equinox really is) either on a full moon or within one week after it (during the third quarter). Thus, the properties discussed earlier with regard to the full moon or the third quarter would apply to Easter.

Good Friday occurs two days prior to Easter and therefore falls within a similar period in the moon's cycle. Neither of these Christian holidays would fall within the

vast majority of the first, second, or fourth quarters (although either could occur at the end of the second quarter on or near the full moon, or around the third quarter moon as the fourth quarter starts).

Like Bill Best, Myrtle Turner's mother planted beans on Good Friday, and Della Shepherd mentioned this as a good bean-planting day as well. Gary Easton's father always planted his potatoes on Good Friday. Susana Lein calls this "the Kentucky old-timers' [practice of] planting by the moon. You know, they would always plant on Good Friday. Because that's when the full moon starts." None of the interviewees stated that Good Friday is not a good planting day. Many almanacs and calendars recognize Good Friday but don't include any specifics about whether it is a good planting day (rather, they rely on the zodiac signs and the phase of the moon for that day). It seems that Good Friday is more of a seasonal reminder, but it is interesting that it always occurs within a week after the full moon.

Maria Thun's research found the opposite to be true: "From Good Friday to Easter Sunday we do not work in the garden at all. In numerous trials we have repeatedly found that garden work of any kind during this period, including harvest, does plants and people no good. Fewer seeds germinate, fruits are smaller, produce quality is diminished and medicinal herbs have less healing power."[21] Once again, this is an area in which the biodynamic calendar clearly differs from the oral tradition and folklore followed in Kentucky and the Appalachian region.

# Valentine's Day

And we planted peas every year on Valentine's Day. That is like a tradition in this area. . . . This year it wasn't in the right sign, but a lot of times during the winter I'll try to make a row in my garden somewhere so that even if it's snowing on Valentine's Day, maybe I can put some peas in just to experiment.

DEBBIE COOK

Valentine's Day was mentioned in two interviews as the time to plant peas. Obviously, this falls on the same date every year and thus wouldn't necessarily correspond to a certain moon phase. For many, it seems to represent the beginning of the gardening season and a reminder to get the peas in early. As Myrtle Turner explains, "Now peas can't stand hot weather . . . they just can't take hot weather. You always plant the peas early, ya know, Valentine's Day is when you're supposed to plant 'em." Phil Case heard from one person that Presidents' Day is when you want to have your peas in, which is very close to Valentine's Day. As any gardener knows, February can still be very cold, but occasional warmth and the lengthening days bring the promise of spring. It makes sense that a marker of the beginning of planting season would persist in oral tradition. Although Valentine's Day is one of the holidays listed in most almanacs and calendars, none offer an opinion about whether planting should occur. They treat the date like all others, with planting recommendations based on the moon's phase and zodiac sign.

Kale and peas.
(Photo by Sarah Hall)

# Ember Days

Now the really killing days would be if you hit . . . an ember day and a day that's a killing sign. An ember day on a Leo or Aries day, I'd stay in the house. I just tell people in my column to stay on the porch.

PHIL CASE

Ember days occur in clusters (on Wednesday, Friday, and Saturday of the same week) four times a year and are designated in liturgical calendars. These are meant to be days of prayer, fasting, and ordination of clergy, according to *The Old Farmer's Almanac*. The origin of these days is somewhat debated, but writings early in the Common Era refer to them, and they were likely tied to agricultural feasts and festivals. Prayer and thanksgiving were important components of early ember day celebrations. Ember days occur following the first Sunday in Lent, Whitsunday-Pentecost, the Feast of the Holy Cross on September 14, and the Feast of St. Lucia on December 13. The latter two fall on specific dates, while the other two are dependent on Easter (and thus can occur over a more than monthlong period). It is worth mentioning that the specific dates sometimes differ between Anglican and Roman Catholic calendars. All almanacs and calendars except for *Llewellyn's Moon Sign Book* specify ember days somewhere. Calendars often include them in the "Best Days" for each month, as determined by the zodiac and phase of the moon (in other words, they don't suggest that those days should be outright avoided). Maria Thun does not discuss them in her work on the biodynamic calendar. *The Old Farmer's Almanac* claims that the weather on each set of ember days forecasts the weather for the next three months.[22]

Everyone who mentioned ember days said that no planting should be done on those days, even if the signs are otherwise favorable. Julie Maruskin explains, "See, that's what's so weird . . . apparently an ember day trumps whatever sign it is. So, it could be in the most fertile sign possible—and it is, this year it's like second quarter Cancer—[but] it falls on an ember day, [so] it's like, well,

Hammock hanging on a porch near the garden.

won't be planting anything on that day. So, I'll be cleaning the house and hoping that works out."

Those who were interviewed highlighted two features of ember days: the ease with which a woody plant can be damaged or killed, and the extreme heat. Plant damage can be enhanced if the ember day falls during one of the killing signs (Aries/Head, Leo/Heart). Gary Easton recounts, "When I was a boy, nine or ten years old, I remember specifically a Saturday that our father [said] . . . the sign was in the Heart . . . and it was [an] ember day, and we took hatchets and he took an axe, my older brother and I, and we went over several acres of our farm then and just [started] hacking on trees because [my father] said that if the sign's in the Heart on [an] ember day we could just hack on a tree and it would eventually die." Jess Clarkson Jr. recalled this feature as well. Goldie Easton mentioned the extreme heat that seemed to occur on ember days during the growing season. She said her parents tried to avoid planting on ember days, but occasionally it couldn't be avoided during the ember days in June. She noted, "You didn't want to be out in the field on an ember day because it just seemed so much hotter."

## Barren Days

*The first three days of May is what they call the barren days. My husband now didn't believe it . . . and he actually planted a row of corn each day. It didn't work, he never got nothin'.*

DELLA SHEPHERD

Two people said the first three days of May are barren days when nothing should be planted—specifically, they both mentioned corn. This reference was not found in any of the published sources. In addition to Della, Clyde Charles recalled, "My dad always said you didn't want to plant corn on the first three days of May, it would be a barren stalk and wouldn't have no ear on it. And I guess I followed [his] footsteps." Like Valentine's Day, because these are set dates on the calendar, they wouldn't be expected to fall in any particular phase of the moon or zodiac sign.

## Women's Connection

*If you go in a cucumber patch when you're on your period, they'll every one die.*

MYRTLE TURNER

It is common knowledge that the average menstrual cycle approximates the cycle of the moon, and many consider this a clear indication that they are closely linked. More than one person interviewed, and several others I've spoken with, stated that one shouldn't do any gardening during menstruation. Sarah Epperson confirms being chased out of the garden by her grandmother Myrtle Turner for that reason, and Sarah shared a photo of some tomatoes and beans that didn't turn out right when she canned them while menstruating. On the flip side, a pregnant woman might be seen as especially fertile, and her presence in the garden might be considered advantageous. This potential benefit was not cited as frequently as the need to avoid the garden during menstruation, but Debbie Cook recalled spending a "long, hot summer" in the garden while pregnant, at the urging of her mother-in-law.

# Beyond Planting

THIS BOOK HAS FOCUSED ON ACTIVITIES RELATED TO gardening and the moon signs, but many other topics came up repeatedly in both the interviews and the published sources. Some sources provide such extensive recommendations that you can plan essentially every aspect of your life by the signs. In this chapter, the most commonly encountered nongardening practices are briefly discussed; almanacs and calendars delve into these practices in greater depth. The information I provide here does not represent my own recommendations.

## FOOD PRESERVATION

An important part of making the bounty of the garden last through the winter is preserving it. Like other aspects of gardening such as planting and harvesting, it is believed that preservation will be most successful if it is performed at certain times. In general, signs that are not good for planting are not good for preserving either, with Virgo/Bowels, Leo/Heart, and Aries/Head being the signs to avoid. The exception to this rule is when drying fruits, vegetables, or meat, in which case the fiery signs of Aries, Leo, and Sagittarius are recommended.[1]

### Sauerkraut and Canning

Well, when we went to make sauerkraut, we always made it on the old moon. It would keep better and stay pretty and white on the old moon.

MARY OVERBEY

Clyde Charles recalled that his mother made kraut "on the last part of the moon" too. Myrtle Turner says, whatever you do, avoid making kraut when the signs are in the Bowels: "If you do kraut when the signs are in the Bowels, it'll turn as dark as it can be, and it'll smell real bad."[2] According to *The Old Farmer's Almanac*, any kind of pickling should be done when the signs are in Scorpio, Pisces, or Cancer. Myrtle Turner adds the Knees (Capricorn) and Thighs (Sagittarius) to this group but says of Pisces, "It's not good to do it in the Feet, 'cause see it's not long til it's going out." She says you don't want to make kraut in the Head (Aries) either. *Baer's Agricultural Almanac* recommends Pisces (Feet) as the appropriate moon sign for making sauerkraut. Maria Thun did trials with sauerkraut and determined that cabbage should be cut and fermentation should be started on flower (Libra, Gemini, Aquarius) or fruit (Aries, Leo, Sagittarius) days.[3]

Most almanacs discuss canning and making sauerkraut together and give similar recommendations for the timing of the two activities. *Llewellyn's Moon Sign Book* cites Scorpio, Cancer, and Pisces as the most favorable signs for canning fruits or vegetables, when they fall in the third or fourth quarter.

**FACING:** Canned and fresh tomatoes.

## ANIMAL HUSBANDRY

When people, you know . . . come through that Depression . . . it was rough. But we lived on a farm, had a big peach orchard and we had stock and would kill hogs and all like that. We lived good, but we didn't have a whole lot of money, you know what I'm sayin', during the Depression. But we made it. My mother would sell chickens and people would come around and buy peaches and chickens from us and all, you know. . . . We done all right.

JESS CLARKSON JR.

Cow and calf grazing in a pasture.

## Weaning and Breaking Bad Habits

And weaning calves, we always try to do the calf weaning when it's down in the Feet. If you don't do that, we might . . . wean twenty-some calves at a time, and all the neighbors will . . . be calling . . . saying, "What . . . are you doing?!" You know, the signs wasn't right. . . . And if it's the wrong sign, you might be three weeks weaning, whereas if it's all the way in the Feet—it's like the mothers [say], it's time for you to go anyway.

JOE TRIGG

Weaning, the process of getting offspring to stop nursing from the mother (typically accomplished by physically separating them), can be stressful for both offspring and mother. Sarah Epperson's notebook containing advice she's heard from others agrees with Joe Trigg that Pisces/Feet is the best time. Many sources include other signs, but they are generally the four signs from the Thighs down (Sagittarius/Thighs, Capricorn/Knees, Aquarius/Legs, and Pisces/Feet), regardless of the moon phase.[4]

Phil Case puts weaning in the general category of making changes, which you want to do when the signs are in the Thighs (Sagittarius) or lower and when the moon is in the dark phase (full to new). Those signs don't rule parts of the body that are essential to function. *The Old Farmer's Almanac* says weaning can be done under the four fruitful signs (Scorpio/Loins, Taurus/Neck, Cancer/Breast, and Pisces/Feet), plus Virgo/Bowels and Capricorn/Knees.

*Llewellyn's Moon Sign Book* treats breaking bad habits separately from weaning and recommends doing so when the moon is in the fourth quarter and in Gemini, Leo, or Aquarius (the barren signs).[5] When Jane Post goes on a raw foods diet, she tries to hit the time favored by *Llewellyn's* for breaking bad habits. *Farmers' Almanac* puts potty training under the same category as weaning and recommends doing it in the same signs (Sagittarius/Thighs down to Pisces/Feet). *The Weather Vane Almanac Calendar* used by Joe Trigg states, "If you want to quit any bad habits do so on the second day that the moon is in the sign of Sagittarius."[6]

## Dehorning and Castrating

You want to do it [dehorning] when it's low . . . when the sign's in the Feet or the Knees. . . . They'll bleed like crazy if you do it when the sign's . . . higher up.

BOBBY CLARKSON

The general rules for weaning seem to hold true for castrating or dehorning animals, with the best signs being Sagittarius/Thighs down through Pisces/Feet. As Walden Whitehead explains, "You got a boar hog . . . [and to] change that hog . . . you gotta catch it going down." *Farmers' Almanac* suggests Sagittarius, Capricorn, Aquarius, and Pisces for castrating. Phil Case recounted a story he heard from his neighbor about castrating hogs: because the signs were right, according to Mr. Van Meter,

"'We cut all these hogs . . . and they never bled once.'" *The Old Farmer's Almanac* recommends castrating when the moon sign is Aquarius (dehorning is not listed in its "Best Days" table).[7] *Llewellyn's Moon Sign Book* lists the good times for spaying or neutering (castrating) animals and suggests third or fourth quarter Sagittarius (Thighs), Capricorn (Knees), or Pisces (Feet).

## Butchering

Killing hogs. . . . If you don't kill them on the old part of the moon or the last quarter of it, you fry bologna and see [it'll] bow right up. And if you kill a hog like that on the new part of the moon or something like that, it'll bow up just like that and you can't fry it in the skillet 'cause it . . . will pop grease all over you.

WALDEN WHITEHEAD

Killing hogs and cows for food has been an essential tradition among families in the Appalachian region. A number of people mentioned the importance of the moon signs for timing the slaughter of animals. Frank Jenkins says timing is crucial to get a nice full ham that cures well, whereas slaughtering in the wrong sign results in meat that shrinks off the bone and won't cure as well. Clyde Charles recalls, "We didn't kill hogs on the new of the moon either, because they said if you done it on the new moon, that the meat would puff up." Myrtle Turner and Glenn Brown agree, noting that when meat curls up in the pan, it is evidence the animal was slaughtered in the new moon, whereas slaughtering in the old moon results in meat that lays flat as it cooks. The oral tradition is remarkably consistent.[8] Although not all the interviewees could recall the correct phase for slaughtering, they all described the difference between the right and wrong signs in the same way. *The Foxfire Book* states, "Slaughter while the signs are in the knees or feet, and in the last quarter of the moon."[9] *Farmers' Almanac* and the *Weather Vane Almanac Calendar* are generally in line with this oral tradition, listing the day of the full moon and one to two days after as being the best times for slaughtering each month.[10] *The Old Farmer's Almanac* differs and says Scorpio is the best moon sign for slaughtering; the phase doesn't matter.

## GENERAL FARMWORK

Plowing and cultivation are discussed in the previous chapter, but almanacs and interviewees mentioned many other tasks related to farming.

### Fencing

We had to build a lot of fence around our fields to keep cattle in, ya know. . . . They was something to it, 'cause a lot of times you go back through a rural fence and every one of 'em would be shackling. Another time you'd go through 'em and all would be good and solid, ya know.

GLENN BROWN

Digging holes and setting fence posts are important activities with a strong tradition based on following the signs.[11] The general advice is that posts should be set in the old part of the moon (third or fourth quarter) to result in a solid fence. Frank Jenkins explains the difference this way: "If you do it in the wrong time of the moon, you won't be able to get all the dirt back in the hole around the post. If you do [it] at the right time of the moon, you'll have to go get some more dirt to put around there 'cause it packs down so much better." The Eastons mentioned following *The Old Farmer's Almanac* for this activity, which recommends setting fence posts when the moon's sign is in Capricorn (Knees); it does not consider the phase of the moon.[12] According to *Farmers' Almanac*, days when Taurus, Leo, and Aquarius are in the third or fourth quarter are good times to dig post holes.

Joe Trigg talked about the importance of timing when cutting cedar for fence posts. He didn't recall the specific phase or sign but said, "A lot of us use cedar trees for fence posts. And if you cut down at the wrong time, they'll rot. If you cut 'em in the right time, then those posts would stay good twenty, thirty years. . . . I would have to go and ask one of the older farmers . . . [as] a lot of this [is] just folklore stuff and things that they just know." A 1991 *New York Times* article discusses cutting and setting living fence posts and quotes Michael Pettit from eastern Kentucky: "Me and my Grandpap, we'd cut locust for fence posts when the moon was three-quarters full. . . . We'd cut them green, leave the bark on and put them right in the ground. Then Grandpap would pour about a gallon of water on them. And a month later those posts would be sprouting. That's no lie, ma'am."[13]

## Spreading Gravel

If you pour gravel when the moon's in the light phase, it . . . stays on top of the ground. If you pour in the dark phase, it sinks . . . it's just the gravitational forces of the moon. Because we have roads on our farm that I had, I poured gravel on, and the whole time before we sold the farm and moved back to town the gravel was right there . . . and then in the next paddock, did it on a different day, and I guess I wasn't paying any attention. You couldn't find a rock. It just all went under.

PHIL CASE

If gravitational pull is an advantage when setting a solid fence post, the opposite is true when spreading gravel—when the goal is for the gravel to stay on the surface. Phil Case advises his readers and followers to spread gravel in any zodiac sign as long as the moon is in the light phase. Frank Jenkins uses the same formula for laying stepping-stones or doing other stone masonry work. *The Old Farmer's Almanac* has an entry in its "Best Days" table for when to "begin logging, set posts, pour concrete"— activities that are universally recommended to be undertaken when the moon sign is Capricorn (Knees).

Flowers growing next to a pasture.

Garden-side studio,
Letcher County.

## Working with Wood

*When you split out your shake shingles, then you put them on. If you put
them on [in] the wrong sign, time of the moon, they'll curl up.*

**FRANK JENKINS**

The moisture content of wood can vary dramatically, so many tasks involving wood
are said to be influenced by the moon's phase. Shake shingles, for example, are supposed to be laid during the dark of the moon.[14] Most printed sources give the same
window (third and fourth quarters) for cutting firewood.[15] *Baer's Agricultural Almanac* says, "The timber cut in the old of the moon in August will not be eaten by
worms nor snap in burning, and will last much longer than timber cut at any other

time."[16] *Llewellyn's Moon Sign Book* agrees: "Timber cut during the waning Moon does not become worm-eaten; it will season well and not warp, decay, or snap during burning. Cut when the Moon is in Taurus, Gemini, Virgo, or Capricorn—especially in August. Avoid the water signs. Look for favorable aspect to Mars."[17] In contrast, *Farmers' Almanac* recommends the opposite period for cutting firewood, starting at the new moon and ending the day before it is full.

## Cutting Hay

The subject of cutting hay did not come up in the interviews but is mentioned in a number of printed sources. Like wood, hay's moisture content is important for proper drying and curing and is influenced by moisture in the soil as well as in the air (humidity). *The Old Farmer's Almanac* cites Aries (Head)—a fiery/dry sign—as best for cutting hay, with the moon's phase being irrelevant. One person interviewed for *The Foxfire Book*, Elvin Cabe, recounted that hay cut "on th' old of th' moon . . . it'll dry a third quicker than it will on th' new."[18] None of the other almanacs or calendars specifically reference when hay should be cut. Louise Riotte discusses the harvesting of grains and says, "Always take care to do this under one of the dry signs and in the third or fourth quarter."[19]

# FISHING

*If you're a fisher person or whatever, then, you know, sometimes the fish just don't bite. So, you know, if I were a fishing person these days, I would probably go along with the moon sign thing.*

JANE POST

All the almanacs rank fishing days, typically on a three- or four-point scale (best, good, fair, poor). Many also state which part of the day is the best—morning or evening. Most almanacs provide these rankings in a separate "Best Days" table, while the calendars either list the best fishing days for each month or sometimes provide a pictorial representation on each calendar day. *Farmers' Almanac* lists many days in the signs of Scor-

pio, Cancer, Pisces, and Aquarius as among the best days to fish; although some days in those four signs are categorized as only good or fair, none are deemed poor. Conversely, Aries, Gemini, Leo, and Sagittarius—all barren/dry signs—are routinely ranked as poor for fishing, or in some cases fair. Libra is also in this less than favorable category. All the other signs fall somewhere in the middle, according to *Farmers' Almanac*.

*The Old Farmer's Almanac* does not specify good fishing days based on astrological signs. Instead, it has one page devoted to the best fishing days and times and provides a number of different formulas that can be used to ensure success (such as one hour before and after low and high tides or during a full moon). The only specific dates deemed the best for fishing are the days between the new and full moon. *Llewellyn's Moon Sign Book* provides a number of general formulas as well. It suggests the best time to fish during the month is the day after the full moon, as well as the days when the moon changes quarters, especially if that day is in a water sign. On any day, the best times to fish are at sunrise plus three hours after and from two hours before sunset to one hour after.

## MEDICAL PROCEDURES

This topic came up both in the interviews and in published references. The general idea is based on medical astrology, although there are differences in interpretations and understandings.

### Surgery

> So, if you have that sequence—when the dark moon's in force and the sign's in the Thighs, the Knees, the Legs, the Feet—those four signs. And they are the best times for elective surgery.
>
> PHIL CASE

There seems to be some debate over when surgery is recommended. A calendar from the American Calendar Company says, "The part of our body governed by a particular constellation is supposed to be more sensitive when the moon is in that constellation." This statement seems to agree with what I heard during the interviews—that is, avoid having surgery when the sign is in or near the body part being operated on. However, the *Weather Vane Almanac Calendar* says, "When the moon resides in various signs certain influences are greater thus surgery performed at that time could have a better time for healing." This is followed by a list of the signs and their corresponding body parts, preceded by the words "healing of" or "healing for." In other words, this calendar suggests scheduling procedures when the sign corresponds to the relevant body part.

*Llewellyn's Moon Sign Book* recommends scheduling surgery for the week before or after a new moon, or when the moon is increasing. It also states: "Select a date when the Moon is past the sign governing the part of the body in the operation. . . . The further removed the Moon sign is from the sign ruling the afflicted part of the body, the better."[20] It then gives more specific guidelines related to planetary aspects and the individual's sun sign. Frank Vinson, interviewed for *Foxfire 11,* said surgery should not be done when the signs are in the Heart, as that would increase bleeding.[21] Interestingly, neither *The Old Farmer's Almanac* nor *Farmers' Almanac* provides any guidance on surgery. Both contain only general wording accompanying their depiction of the almanac man and state that astrologers believed each astrological sign had an effect on or influence over those parts of the body.[22]

## Dental Work

My brother-in-law, when he had his wisdom teeth cut out, I told him not to do it because the signs were in the Neck, and he did it anyway, but he bled for like a week and a half. And when I had mine done, they were in the Knees, and I was good.

SARAH EPPERSON

Dental procedures, particularly having teeth pulled or removed, were mentioned in the interviews and in numerous publications. According to *The Old Farmer's Almanac*, dental procedures should be done when the signs are in Virgo. *Llewellyn's Moon Sign Book* also recommends Virgo for having teeth removed, as well as Gemini, Sagittarius, or Pisces during the first or second quarter.[23] Phil Case's recommendations for dental procedures are the same as for surgery: Sagittarius/Thighs down through Pisces/Feet, when the moon is in the dark phase. Myrtle Turner says, "Same way when you have your teeth pulled. Go by your signs. Don't do it in the Head, 'cause

I had it done [in the Head] and I had to go and have mine packed 'cause they liked to bled me to death." Mary Overbey and Walden Whitehead agree not to have dental work when the signs are in the Head, and Walden specifies they should be in the Knees or lower. Julie Maruskin recounted a conversation with coworkers about scheduling a root canal and said fourth quarter Sagittarius is considered a good time. She said of her coworker, "And he didn't [bleed much]. And he's a bleeder."

## WEATHER

[The predictions are] pretty close, you know, on frost dates and unexpected [weather]. Again, I'm making the assumption that whoever's interpreting the data, they're saying, "Hey, the moon will be here, this is where it's been at for thousands of years, [and] when it's at this location and it's at this space, this is what potentially can happen." And then the weatherman'll say, "Oh, we've got a surprise," ya know, and a lot of times the farmer's almanac . . . is sayin', "Hey, you morons." So, we're looking at . . . hey, the farmer's almanac says it's going to be a problem, so we're coverin' up [our plants]. . . . Then you wake up the next morning and it's, you know, you got frost on your vehicles.

JOE TRIGG

Weather predictions are perhaps the most ubiquitous information in both calendars and almanacs. The formulations vary by printed source and are not described in any way, so it is unclear whether the moon's zodiac signs or phases are incorporated. Every source claims to be the best, and each has its own meteorologist who makes the predictions based on time-tested calculations. Given the importance of the weather for all outdoor activities, including farming and gardening, it is no surprise that such information is considered useful. In most cases, there are both general forecasts for the different regions of the United States separated by seasons and more specific forecasts within each month. Many calendars feature a symbol to represent the daily forecast. Most meteorologists do not subscribe to such fine-tuned extended weather predictions. These predictions really just aim to refine the initial observations made by astrologers millennia ago, which formed the basis of understanding seasonal rhythms and establishing calendar systems.

# Epilogue

We who are constantly searching realize, with humility, just how much we still must learn.

LOUISE RIOTTE, *Planetary Planting*

Much of this book was written during the COVID-19 pandemic. This period in our history gave many people time to think about what matters most. In the United States, the shutdown coincided with spring gardening season, and this activity became an outlet for many (myself included). Compost was sold out in many places by early April 2020. Seed companies reported record sales due to "pandemic gardening." As the summer brought bountiful harvests, a black market of sorts developed for canning supplies. A virus that thrived in our interconnected world retaught many of us about the beauty and peace that come from raising our own food from the soil beneath our feet.

I have had a garden for the last fifteen years. Although I am pretty horrible when it comes to maintaining house plants, there is something about nurturing a plant, seeing it produce food, and then eating that food that I find incredibly comforting. In some years, my garden has been only a couple of small raised beds; in others, I've had a combination of rows in the ground and raised beds. My pandemic garden had more varieties of vegetable crops and far fewer weeds than I've ever been able to pull off. And of course, it felt sacrilegious not to look at the calendar and at least make notes of what and when I planted.

## LESSONS LEARNED

I learned that planting by the signs requires patience. There will be many days that are perfect for planting in every other way, but you have to resist the temptation because the signs aren't right. Still, there are always plenty of other things to do in the garden: weeding, mulching, and preparing the ground; sifting through your seed box and planning what will go where. There will be days when the signs are right but the soil moisture or the weather isn't. Many gardeners, however, don't hesitate to wade through the mud to plant when the sign is right (including Louise Riotte, as she states on the first page of *Planetary Planting*) or to plant by headlamp, which I found myself doing. You may hear about other people putting their crops in before you do, or perhaps, if you're less cautious than I am, you'll find yourself planting before others are doing so. It's especially hard to miss out on a good sign because of bad weather and then have to wait another fourteen days for a favorable day (this happens when the favorable sign occurs in the second and fourth quarters).

Planting by the signs requires an awareness of the calendar not just as it relates to the moon signs but also as it relates to your personal schedule, the weather forecast, the preparation that needs to be done, and the like. Planting by the signs requires a good deal of planning.

I also learned from experience that different calendars can vary by 1.5 days or so in their zodiac sign designations. The best strategy seems to be to pick one calendar and stick with it. If you use more than one calendar, you can try to hit the window that is best in both, but this trims a two- to three-day window down to an even narrower one, and cross-referencing the two calendars can be confusing.

Although I observed how quickly soil conditions can change, I didn't necessarily make note of this on my calendar. As someone who understands soil moisture and porosity on a scientific level, I can say that the changes and their rapidity didn't always seem to be merely the result of precipitation and the sun's (daily) influence. Soil that is quite pliable and moist can quickly become extremely dry. As I noticed this, I couldn't help thinking about Steiner's view that the moon's influence on the earth is mediated by water, and I wondered whether the moon's position could be responsible for such dramatic changes.

I also can't help feeling incredibly lucky to have met all those who shared their time and wisdom with me for this project. Whenever I would be tempted to plant sweet corn, I could hear Debbie Cook saying, "Plantin' corn! Plantin' corn!" as she described her mother-in-law's interpretation of the cawing crows. A similar lesson came to mind when I recalled Susana Lein having to replant her corn three times and hang CDs all over her garden to keep the birds out. (For now, I'm happy to keep supporting other farmers' corn endeavors by putting it in my grocery cart or in my shopping bag at the farmers' market. But if I ever do venture into corn, I'll be sure to have one of my boys out there covering up each corn seed quickly to thwart any nearby crows as I tell him Debbie's story.) And as I weeded around each tomato plant while waiting on water from the hose, I couldn't help but think of Della Shepherd saying over and over, "It's simple. It's just little things." And I remembered Walden Whitehead talking about the hard work of gardening, saying, "By the time you go to bed, you'll stay there."

## MY RESULTS

I can easily say that my pandemic garden was the best I've ever had. There were obviously a lot of variables, so this was in no way a controlled experiment. My bush beans planted in Scorpio/Loins/Secrets were amazingly productive, although one variety (Derby) clearly did better than the other (Contender), which didn't germinate consistently. The pole beans I planted in Gemini/Arms (one of Bill Best's heirlooms) did very well. Carrots planted in fourth quarter Cancer in August resulted in a wonderful fall harvest.

I had some failures, too. Some of these crops were planted in less than favorable signs (broccoli and cabbage starts planted during Sagittarius), but others were planted in good signs (beets in fourth quarter Taurus). On a new moon day in Cancer, my husband planted melons and I planted pole beans—and neither did much of anything (perhaps the influences *were* confused).[1] Cucumbers transplanted in fourth quarter Pisces were extremely abundant (despite being planted in the phase designated for root rather than aboveground crops). The reasons for these successes and failures will remain a mystery. Of course, when you purchase seedlings, there's no way of knowing when the seeds were planted, so perhaps that played a role. And then there are the many other variables that anyone who gardens must contend with. Or perhaps these successes and failures really were attributable to the signs.

I think one of the reasons planting by the signs can confer success is that it encourages succession planting—that is, making numerous plantings of the same

Bill Best's North Carolina speckled greasy cut-shorts. (Photo by Sarah Hall)

crop over time to obtain longer production. Because the good windows are narrow, it can be quite difficult (especially for those who can't garden full time) to plant everything at once. This means you plant some beans (or whatever) and then wait six or fourteen days for another good sign before planting some more. If you garden like I do, you're also more likely to look in your seed box and find a different variety to plant at the next good sign, so you end up planting both in succession and with more diversity. This makes success more likely than if you plant only one variety of each vegetable on a single day (especially if that one day isn't in a good sign).

## TRY IT YOURSELF

If you are curious and would like to try planting by the signs, reading this book has put you well on your way. Now you'll need a calendar to follow, which can be in hard copy or online. If you are on Facebook, you can find Phil Case's "Planting by the Signs" page and like it to follow his updates, or look for the page on Twitter @plantingbysigns. In general, calendars and almanacs come out in the fall for the following year. (If you are lucky enough to know some local businesses that sell their own calendars or give them away, don't wait until March or April to try to find one.) Farmer's almanacs require some reading and a bit of deciphering, but you should now be well equipped to do so.

For an easy-to-understand calendar, I recommend *Gardening by the Moon* by Caren Catterall.[2] Businesses sometimes offer *Farmers' Almanac* for free or purchase, and *The Old Farmer's Almanac* is widely available for purchase. If you want to really dig in and get advice about when to do everything, *Llewellyn's Moon Sign Book* is a great choice. It has tons of information about the *how* as well as a bit of the *why,* along with detailed weekly calendars with transition periods, planetary aspects, weather predictions, and so on. Biodynamics is an agricultural religion of sorts, and if you're more interested in the astronomical than the astrological, you might want to consult the *Stella Natura* calendar or *The Maria Thun Biodynamic Almanac.*

Once you have made your choice, dive in and see what it has to offer! As you garden, keep records, which can constitute your own experiments. Your successes will be measured in delicious harvests from your garden, and even failures mean that you got out in the garden, which is always time well spent.

## FINAL THOUGHT

I thank you for taking the time to read this book. If you are interested in learning more, I hope you will listen to the recorded interviews, available via the Berea College Special Collection and Archives website (see the bibliography). While I have given voice to those interviewed, there is no substitute for their own voices, and every single one of them is well worth the listen.

Bountiful September harvest. (Photo by Sarah Hall)

# Acknowledgments

JUST AS EACH PLANT IN THE GARDEN NEEDS support and nourishment from many sources (the soil and the life within it, water, neighboring plants, the gardener), I too could never have completed this work on my own. First and foremost are those I interviewed; our time together rejuvenated me (both professionally and personally) in a way that is hard to put into words. Thanks also to Berea College and the Kentucky Oral History Commission, which helped fund this work. Meg Wilson spent hours with me on the backroads of Kentucky as we traveled to the interviews, and she created the beautiful photographs in this book. It is hard to imagine this project without them, and I'm sure you, as a reader, can appreciate the rich documentation they provide. During the writing process, Sam Cole was an amazing help to me as I found my footing in this type of writing. She gave her time and energy and offered encouragement when I needed it most. Heather Dent (artwork) and Melissa Strobel (handwriting) graciously contributed their time and effort to make the illustrations truly special. A number of folks at the University Press of Kentucky were instrumental in shepherding this project through what ended up being a five-year process. There are surely many whose names and roles I don't know, but here are those I do: Patrick O'Dowd provided continual patience, support, and reassurance. Tatianna Verswyvel came up with the excellent title. Ila McEntire helped to manage numerous details that transformed words and images into this book. Jackie Wilson's efforts to promote the book will undoubtedly get it into the hands of many more than if it were just left up to me. And finally, the support of my husband, Jake Royse, enabled me to work countless evenings and weekends.

# Notes

## INTRODUCTION

1. Berea College is a private liberal arts college located in Berea, Kentucky. Founded by the abolitionist John G. Fee in 1855, it was the first interracial and coeducational school in the South. All students take part in a work-study program to offset their tuition, and only students with limited financial means are admitted. More information can be found at Berea.edu.

2. Appalshop, based in Whitesburg, Kentucky, began as a community film workshop in 1969 and has grown into a flourishing source of media production in eastern Kentucky and other parts of Appalachia. See, for example, the films *Catfish: Man of the Woods, Nature's Way, Minnie Black's Gourd Band, Oaksie,* and *Sarah Bailey, Chairmaker.* For more information, visit Appalshop.org.

3. See the Appalshop films *Applewise, Grassroots Small Farm,* and *Mountain Farmer.*

4. Eliot Wigginton, ed., *The Foxfire Book* (Garden City, NY: Anchor Press/Doubleday, 1972), 212–27; Kaye Carver Collins and Lacy Hunter, eds., *Foxfire 11: The Old Homeplace, Wild Plant Uses, Preserving and Cooking Food, Hunting Stories, Fishing, and More Affairs of Plain Living* (New York: Anchor Books, 1999), 60–63. The Foxfire series of books grew out of a project started in 1966 by a teacher in northeastern Georgia. He had his students interview their families and friends and document their skills and knowledge. The magazine resulting from that project, which documented the cultural history of numerous residents of Georgia and beyond, was later turned into a series of twelve books. Other teachers became involved in the project and edited later magazines and books. For more information, go to foxfire.org.

5. Gerald Milnes, *Signs, Cures & Witchery: German Appalachian Folklore* (Knoxville: University of Tennessee Press, 2012), 24, 85.

6. David Cooke, email message to the author, November 9, 2017. Grow Appalachia is part of Berea College's Strategic Initiatives and can best be described as an extension-type program aimed at supporting food security in Appalachia. It was started in 2009. More information can be found at growappalachia.berea.edu.

7. See, for example, J. R. Gower, *Gwydion's Planting Guide: The Definitive Moon-Planting Manual* (Glastonbury, UK: J. R. Gower, 1994); Matt Jackson, *Lunar & Biodynamic Gardening* (New York: CICO Books, 2015); "Planting by Moon Signs," *African Violet Magazine* 62, no. 4 (2009): 56–57; Jen Reise-

man, ed., *Planting by the Moon: Folklore for Today's Gardener* (n.p.: Rodale, 2000); Wigginton, *Foxfire Book,* 213.

8. See Milnes, *Signs, Cures & Witchery,* chapter 5.

9. Caren Catterall, *Gardening by the Moon* (Guerneville, CA: Divine Inspiration Publications, 2017).

10. Kurt Holtzknecht and Ernst Zürcher, "Tree Stems and Tides—A New Approach and Elements of Reflexion," *Schweizerische Zeitschrift Forstwesen* 157 (2006): 185–90; K. Steppe, R. Lemeur, and R. Samson, "Sap Flow Dynamics of a Beech Tree during the Solar Eclipse of 11 August 1999," *Agricultural and Forest Meteorology* 112 (2002): 139–49; Peter Barlow, "Moon and Cosmos: Plant Growth and Plant Bioelectricity," in *Plant Electrophysiology,* ed. A. G. Volkov (New York: Springer, 2012), 249–80.

11. Maria Thun, *Results from the Biodynamic Sowing and Planting Calendar* (Edinburgh: Floris, 2003).

# THE BASICS

1. There are earlier records, such as bone carvings and cave paintings depicting celestial bodies, dating back at least 25,000 years.

2. The other major means of communication from the gods was believed to occur through physical marks or imperfections in the livers of animals that were sacrificed.

3. Astrology persisted in those Christian areas, but it could not be practiced openly without fear of retribution.

4. The *Enuma Anu Enlil* is a collection of about seventy clay tablets containing cuneiform omens. The predictions in these tablets are broad and do not relate to individual persons (other than kings) or behaviors. Each tablet has numerous omens (the total is estimated at 7,000), and to date, less than half have been translated and published.

5. At that time, it was believed that the sun revolved around the earth, but the plane was the same.

6. Derived from the ancient Greek *zoion,* for "animals," with *zodiac* translating as "cycle of animals."

7. The name *sidereal* is derived from the Latin *sidus,* meaning "star."

8. The Greek *tropicos* means "belonging to a turn," reflecting the importance of the sun's path (or turn) relative to the earth.

9. Recalling that each sign constitutes 30 degrees of the 365-degree zodiac pie, this means that the two systems will differ in 23 of the 30 degrees. This is the difference given in Aaron Lawrence, ed., *Llewellyn's 2018 Moon Sign Book* (Woodbury, MN: Llewellyn Publications, 2017).

10. Which constellations are included depends on how close they are to the ecliptic and their size. Janice Stillman, ed., *The Old Farmer's Almanac* (Dublin, NH: Yankee Publishing, 2018), includes Auriga, Cetus, Orion, and Sextans (in addition to Ophiucus).

11. Exact estimates of the length of the moon's cycle vary. According to the American Calendar Company, it is 29.5 days; according to Lawrence, *Llewellyn's 2018 Moon Sign Book,* it is 27.33 days.

12. This is true because the moon completes exactly one rotation on its axis during one revolution or orbit around the earth.

13. According to Lawrence, *Llewellyn's 2018 Moon Sign Book*.

14. To understand the concept of retrograde, imagine passing a slow-moving truck on the interstate. From your perspective, the truck appears to be going backward for a short time as you pass it.

15. In figure 1.1, the moon has just entered the descending node and will remain there until it is aligned (approximately) with Aries, at which time it will become ascending.

16. Many studies have examined the correlation between the moon's cycle and menstruation as well as births. A handful of short-term, small-scale studies found a correlation, but those with larger samples (and often longer time frames or broader geographic regions) did not.

17. Louise Riotte, *Planetary Planting* (New York: Simon & Schuster, 1975), 12 (emphasis in original).

18. The *Astronomica* or *Astronomicum* is a Latin poem comprising five books, believed to be written by Roman poet Marcus Manilius (circa 30–40 CE). The zodiac is covered in the second and third books, including an association with body parts.

19. For example, Easter is the first Sunday following the full moon that occurs on or just after the vernal (spring) equinox.

20. For an excellent discussion of religious beliefs and their roots among the original European settlers in Appalachia, as well as their continued presence today, see Gerald Milnes, *Signs, Cures & Witchery: German Appalachian Folklore* (Knoxville: University of Tennessee Press, 2012).

21. Anatomically, the human liver has either two or four lobes, depending on how it is viewed (from above, two lobes; from below, four). It is likely that the two smaller lobes were viewed as one at the time this plant was named.

22. Dennis Horn and Tavia Cathcart, eds., *Wildflowers of Tennessee, the Ohio Valley and the Southern Appalachians* (Auburn, WA: Lone Pine Publishing, 2013), 60.

23. This is also stated in Eliot Wigginton, ed., *The Foxfire Book* (Garden City, NY: Anchor Press/Doubleday, 1972).

24. Della Shepherd, telephone conversation with the author.

25. See Nandi's comment on Tipper, "Planting by the Signs," *Blind Pig & the Acorn,* March 12, 2019, https://blindpigandtheacorn.com/planting-by-the-signs-3/.

## THE FOLLOWERS

1. Despite much searching—and many hours of scanning microfilms by a very dedicated librarian at Kentucky State University—the columns that covered The Great Tomato Project could not be located.

2. The calendar, written by Caren D. Catterall, is available from https://www.gardeningbythemoon.com.

3. For Bill Best's seed-saving efforts, see https://www.heirlooms.org.

4. Biodynamics is discussed briefly in the next chapter. It encompasses much more than the calendar, and Susana has found it especially helpful in composting and in the use of field sprays to activate soil microbial life.

5. Bill Best, *Kentucky Heirloom Seeds: Growing, Eating, Saving* (Lexington: University Press of Kentucky, 2017), 199–207.

# ALMANACS AND CALENDARS

1. For a brief story of how *The Old Farmer's Almanac* came to be, see Janice Stillman et al., "The Life and Times of Robert B. Thomas: Starting *The Old Farmer's Almanac*," April 21, 2020, https://www.almanac.com/extra/life-and-times-robert-b-thomas.

2. *Old* was added to the title in 1847, when Thomas died and his successor John H. Jenks took over as editor.

3. These constellations are Auriga, Cetus, Orion, Sextans, and Ophiucus.

4. The publisher states that astronomical information is "carefully calculated for the Meridian of Pennsylvania and the adjoining States by Hart Wright Company, Lewiston, Maine, with Weather Predictions for the U.S., Sun and Moon Tables, and additional astronomical information for all parts of the nation. Inquiries about astronomical data should be mailed direct to Hart Wright Company."

5. Julie Maruskin referenced this almanac.

6. Aaron Lawrence, ed., *Llewellyn's 2018 Moon Sign Book* (Woodbury, MN: Llewellyn Publications, 2017), 133.

7. Rudolf Steiner was prolific throughout his lifetime, writing and teaching that his belief system applied to all areas of study. He is also well known for establishing the system of education the Waldorf schools follow.

8. Libra is shortest (at twenty-nine hours per cycle) and Virgo is longest (at seventy-seven hours per cycle). Very little of the constellational zodiac overlaps with either the sidereal or the tropical astrological zodiac.

9. The North American edition of *The Maria Thun Biodynamic Almanac* is printed by Floris Books.

10. The *Stella Natura* biodynamic calendar is edited by Sherry Wildfeuer and has been published by Camphill Village Kimberton Hills since 1978.

11. No longer available is the Cardui calendar (which displayed two months per sheet), put out by the Chattanooga Medicine Company (renamed the Chattem Drug and Chemical Company in 1966) of Chattanooga, Tennessee. Production ended in 2012, after 122 years.

12. Black quoted in Eliot Wigginton, ed., *The Foxfire Book* (Garden City, NY: Anchor Press/Doubleday, 1972), 213. *The Ladies Birthday Almanac* was produced by the Chattanooga Medicine Company (formerly the Chattem Drug and Chemical Company) from 1890 to 2012 to promote its products.

13. Louise Riotte, *Planetary Planting* (New York: Simon & Schuster, 1975), endorses *Llewellyn's Moon Sign Book* as a reliable almanac.

14. Riotte, *Planetary Planting*, 36.

# THE SIGNS

1. In addition to Glenn Brown, this was mentioned by Clyde Charles, Mary Overbey, Myrtle Turner, Walden Whitehead, and Frank Jenkins.

2. Caren Catterall's *Gardening by the Moon* calendar states that full moon and new moon days should be avoided "because the influences are somewhat confused as the tides turn" (back cover).

3. This is stated in Aaron Lawrence, ed., *Llewellyn's 2018 Moon Sign Book* (Woodbury, MN: Llewellyn Publications, 2017), and it coincides with the advice in the *Gardening by the Moon* calendar as well. According to *Llewellyn's 2018 Moon Sign Book,* one exception to this general rule is cucumbers, which are said to do better when planted in the first quarter.

4. For instance, Julie Maruskin says, "You don't want to try to plant anything in fourth quarter Leo because it'll burn up."

5. Louise Riotte, *Planetary Planting* (New York: Simon & Schuster, 1975).

6. Black quoted in Eliot Wigginton, ed., *The Foxfire Book* (Garden City, NY: Anchor Press/Doubleday, 1972), 213. All Black's recommendations cited in this chapter are from the same source.

7. Bill Best, *Kentucky Heirloom Seeds: Growing, Eating, Saving* (Lexington: University Press of Kentucky, 2017); Ronni Lundy, *Victuals* (New York: Clarkson Potter, 2016).

8. Wigginton, *Foxfire Book;* Kaye Carver Collins and Lacy Hunter, eds., *Foxfire 11: The Old Homeplace, Wild Plant Uses, Preserving and Cooking Food, Hunting Stories, Fishing, and More Affairs of Plain Living* (New York: Anchor Books, 1999).

9. Riotte, *Planetary Planting,* suggests harvesting fruit and roots for storage in Leo; two other sources suggest harvesting more generally.

10. Catterall, *Gardening by the Moon* calendar.

11. Anything planted in Virgo will result in lots of flowers but very little fruit. Riotte, *Planetary Planting,* says flowers planted in this sign will be abundant.

12. Catterall, *Gardening by the Moon* calendar.

13. Catterall, *Gardening by the Moon* calendar.

14. Nancy Tappan, ed., *Harris Farmer's Almanac* (Nashville, TN: Athlon Publications, 2020). The recommendation to plant flowers in Aquarius occurs in only one month, so it may be dictated by something other than the sign.

15. *The Weather Vane Almanac Calendar* (2019) contains no publisher information. It was obtained at the Southern States Glasgow Co-Op.

16. As previously discussed, T. E. Black considers Aquarius a good sign.

17. For the Northern Hemisphere, this date is the official start of spring, whereas in the Southern Hemisphere, it marks the beginning of autumn. Centuries ago, March 21 was designated the date of the ecclesiastical equinox to simplify the calculation of Easter's occurrence, even though the actual equinox falls within a three-day window.

18. The vernal equinox is also the marker for 0-degrees Aries in both the tropical and sidereal zodiac systems. The tropical system adjusts for the precession of the equinoxes, while the sidereal does not.

19. A full moon occurs on the vernal equinox only every nineteen years.

20. There is quite a debate surrounding the date of Easter, and not all Christians agree. The date depends on whether the Julian or Gregorian calendar is used, which differs between Eastern and Western Christian traditions. Further debate centers around the calculation of the moon phases and the vernal equinox. Some believe the calculation should be centered on astronomical observations—in some cases, from certain locations—rather than the systems used by calendar makers, which do not necessarily align with the astronomical occurrence.

21. Maria Thun, *The Biodynamic Year: Increasing Yield, Quality and Flavor* (Malta: Temple Lodge, 2007), 12.

22. Wednesday's weather forecasts the month that follows, Friday forecasts the second month, and Saturday forecasts the third month.

## BEYOND PLANTING

1. Janice Stillman, ed., *The Old Farmer's Almanac* (Dublin, NH: Yankee Publishing, 2018).

2. The same is said by Leona Carver in Kaye Carver Collins and Lacy Hunter, eds., *Foxfire 11: The Old Homeplace, Wild Plant Uses, Preserving and Cooking Food, Hunting Stories, Fishing, and More Affairs of Plain Living* (New York: Anchor Books, 1999), 62.

3. Maria Thun, *The Biodynamic Year: Increasing Yield, Quality and Flavor* (Malta: Temple Lodge, 2007), 89. Because the biodynamic calendar relies on the astronomical zodiac, it does not overlap with other calendars.

4. These sources include Aaron Lawrence, ed., *Llewellyn's 2018 Moon Sign Book* (Woodbury, MN: Llewellyn Publications, 2017); Peter Geiger and Sandi Duncan, eds., *Farmers' Almanac* (Lewiston, ME: Almanac Publishing Company, 2020); *Weather Vane Almanac Calendar*; and my interview with Frank Jenkins.

5. Aries, Virgo, and Capricorn may be suitable as well, but it depends on the habit. Make sure your lunar cycle is favorable, and avoid lunar aspects to Mars or Jupiter. Lawrence, *Lewellyn's 2018 Moon Sign Book,* 18.

6. *The Weather Vane Almanac Calendar* does not list a publisher. Joe Trigg obtained it from Southern States Glasgow Co-op.

7. Apparently, the moon's phase doesn't matter. *The Old Farmer's Almanac* simply lists all Aquarius days for each month as being good for castrating.

8. Eliot Wigginton, ed., *The Foxfire Book* (Garden City, NY: Anchor Press/Doubleday, 1972), 224, also describes this outcome.

9. Wigginton, 219.

10. This means that, over the course of the year, essentially all the zodiac signs are listed.

11. Some references also discuss digging graves, with the same outcome as for fence posts: dirt will be left over in the new moon but not in the old moon. Wigginton, *Foxfire Book,* discusses both setting posts (221–22) and digging graves (226–27).

12. *The Old Farmer's Almanac* combines logging and pouring concrete with digging fence posts in its "Best Days" table.

13. Anne Raver, "Planting by the Full Moon: Bright Idea, or Lunacy?" *New York Times,* May 2, 1991.

14. In his interview, Frank Jenkins referenced the book *A Little Better than Plumb* by Henry and Janice Holt Giles, which describes the building of a log cabin. On two separate occasions, shingles laid when the moon was in the light phase curled up. When they were finally laid in the dark phase, they stayed flat.

15. Wigginton, *Foxfire Book,* 221.

16. Linda Weidman, ed., *Baer's 2019 Agricultural Almanac* (Lancaster, PA: John Baer's Sons, 2018), 78.

17. Lawrence, *Llewellyn's 2018 Moon Sign Book,* 112–13.

18. Wigginton, *Foxfire Book,* 221.

19. Louise Riotte, *Planetary Planting* (New York: Simon & Schuster, 1975), 319.

20. Lawrence, *Llewellyn's 2018 Moon Sign Book,* 127.

21. Collins and Hunter, *Foxfire 11,* 63.

22. The editor of *Farmers' Almanac* says, "The one activity I offer no advice [on] is surgery. Hundreds of years ago, people bled to death during surgery. So, it was important to do it during a time when blood flowed less. Today it is not an issue and, with all the lawyers into the world, I don't dispense medical advice." Peter Geiger, "Use the Signs for Best Days," *Farmers' Almanac,* December 5, 2020, https://www.farmersalmanac.com/use-the-signs-for-best-days-197.

23. Lawrence, *Llewellyn's 2018 Moon Sign Book,* 113.

## EPILOGUE

1. Catterall's *Gardening by the Moon* calendar advises avoiding new and full moon days for this reason.

2. Catterall's *Gardening by the Moon* calendar is available from https://www.gardeningbythemoon.com. There are three versions to match the different growing seasons, so be sure to get the one that corresponds to yours.

# Selected Bibliography

Collins, Kaye Carver, and Lacy Hunter, eds. *Foxfire 11: The Old Homeplace, Wild Plant Uses, Preserving and Cooking Food, Hunting Stories, Fishing, and More Affairs of Plain Living.* New York: Anchor Books, 1999.

Lawrence, Aaron, ed. *Llewellyn's 2018 Moon Sign Book.* Woodbury, MN: Llewellyn Publications, 2017.

Milnes, Gerald. *Signs, Cures & Witchery: German Appalachian Folklore.* Knoxville: University of Tennessee Press, 2012.

Planting by the Signs in Kentucky. Oral History Collection, 2018–2019. Berea College Special Collections and Archives, Berea, KY. https://berea.access.preservica.com/uncategorized/SO_26ded237-7fe5-4d0b-8dd4-0ebd49d10fc2/.

Raver, Anne. "Planting by the Full Moon: Bright Idea, or Lunacy?" *New York Times,* May 2, 1991.

Riotte, Louise. *Planetary Planting.* New York: Simon & Schuster, 1975.

Thun, Maria. *The Biodynamic Year: Increasing Yield, Quality and Flavor.* Malta: Temple Lodge, 2007.

Thun, Maria. *Results from the Biodynamic Sowing and Planting Calendar.* Edinburgh: Floris, 2003.

Wigginton, Eliot, ed. *The Foxfire Book.* Garden City, NY: Anchor Press/Doubleday, 1972.

# Index